T0150860

# Endorsements

"Emily Bernath has a unique way of seeing the world, seeing ourselves, seeing the trials we all face, and seeing our relationship with God. *Broken Lenses* is a powerful, practical guide for bringing clarity and a new, empowering perspective into view. *Broken Lenses* is more than a must-read, it's a must-do for anyone who doubts their worth in the eyes of God."

**Angie Fenimore**, International Bestselling Author and Speaker, and The Calliope Writing Coach

# Broken Lenses

# Broken Lenses

## *Identifying* **YOUR** *Truth in a World of Lies*

## Emily Bernath

NASHVILLE

NEW YORK • LONDON • MELBOURNE • VANCOUVER

# Broken Lenses

## Identifying Your Truth in a World of Lies

© 2020 Emily Bernath

All rights reserved. No portion of this book may be reproduced, stored in a retrieval system, or transmitted in any form or by any means—electronic, mechanical, photocopy, recording, scanning, or other—except for brief quotations in critical reviews or articles, without the prior written permission of the publisher.

Published in New York, New York, by Morgan James Publishing. Morgan James is a trademark of Morgan James, LLC. www.MorganJamesPublishing.com

ISBN 9781642793062 paperback
ISBN 9781642793079 eBook
Library of Congress Control Number: 2018912159

**Cover Design by:**
Rachel Lopez
www.r2cdesign.com

**Interior Design by:**
Christopher Kirk
www.GFSstudio.com

Unless otherwise noted, Scripture is taken from the Good News Bible in Today's English Version—Second Edition Copyright © 1992 by American Bible Society. Used by Permission. All rights reserved.

Scripture quotations marked (NIV) are taken from The Holy Bible, New International Version˚ NIV˚ Copyright © 1973, 1978, 1984, 2011 by Biblica, Inc.˚ Used by permission. All rights reserved worldwide.

Scripture quotations marked (ESV) are from The Holy Bible, English Standard Version, copyright © 2001 by Crossway Bibles, a publishing ministry of Good News Publishers. Used by permission. All rights reserved.

Morgan James is a proud partner of Habitat for Humanity Peninsula and Greater Williamsburg. Partners in building since 2006.

Get involved today! Visit
MorganJamesPublishing.com/giving-back

# Table of Contents

Acknowledgements . . . . . . . . . . . . . . . . . . . . . . . . . . . . . . . . . . . . . . . . . . . . .ix
Introduction . . . . . . . . . . . . . . . . . . . . . . . . . . . . . . . . . . . . . . . . . . . . . . . . . .xi

Chapter One     *I Am Interesting* . . . . . . . . . . . . . . . . . . . . . . . . . . . . . . . 1
Chapter Two     *I Am Creative* . . . . . . . . . . . . . . . . . . . . . . . . . . . . . . . 21
Chapter Three     *I Am Not Alone* . . . . . . . . . . . . . . . . . . . . . . . . . . . . 37
Chapter Four     *I Don't Deserve Happiness* . . . . . . . . . . . . . . . . . . . . . 55
Chapter Five     *I Am Useful* . . . . . . . . . . . . . . . . . . . . . . . . . . . . . . . 71
Chapter Six     *I Am _____ Enough* . . . . . . . . . . . . . . . . . . . . . . . . . 89
Chapter Seven     *I Am Smart* . . . . . . . . . . . . . . . . . . . . . . . . . . . . . . 109
Chapter Eight     *I Have a Purpose* . . . . . . . . . . . . . . . . . . . . . . . . . . 131
Chapter Nine     *I Am Lovable* . . . . . . . . . . . . . . . . . . . . . . . . . . . . . 149
Chapter Ten     *I Am Beautiful* . . . . . . . . . . . . . . . . . . . . . . . . . . . . . 167
Chapter Eleven     *I Am Capable of _____* . . . . . . . . . . . . . . . . . . . . 189
Chapter Twelve     *I Am Not a Failure* . . . . . . . . . . . . . . . . . . . . . . . . . 211

About the Author . . . . . . . . . . . . . . . . . . . . . . . . . . . . . . . . . . . . . . . . . . . . 229
Call to Action . . . . . . . . . . . . . . . . . . . . . . . . . . . . . . . . . . . . . . . . . . . . . . . 231

# Acknowledgements

I can't say I ever dreamed of being an author as a child, reading was never something that I was well-known for. To be honest, I think that has been one of the best parts about the whole process of writing this book. I knew as soon as I felt God calling me to write a book that I would never be able to successfully do it on my own, and I am thankful for all of the help he placed in my path along the way to make this book a reality.

First of all, this book went from just an idea to reality because I had an amazing support group of friends backing me from the very beginning. Thank you Ali, Becky, Chaliece, Danielle, Jordan and Valerie for believing in me and my message, I will forever cherish all of those nights meeting together at my home dearly.

To Angie Fenimore for all of the coaching and wisdom you provided for me along the way. You helped me to see my potential as a writer and to see the potential that this book has for speaking God's light to others. You helped me take this book from something I was writing with the intention of reaching just a small group of people and showed me how it could be so much more than that. Thank you for always believing in me and for speaking truth back into my life when I needed it most. And to Michael Sheen, thank you for all your work put into bringing vision into moving into a career as an author, both with branding and website design.

To my K2 the Church family, thank you for your continued excitement throughout the entire time I've been on this journey of writing this book. It may not seem like a lot in the moment, but even something as simple as just asking how my book writing is going on a Sunday morning provided the motivation to keep going even when the writing got tough. The church is called the body of Christ for a reason, it involves many parts, and all of your prayers as parts of that body have moved mountains to help get me to where I am today.

To all my friends and family back in Ohio, thank you for all of your support from afar. Moving away from you all to pursue life out in Utah was far from an easy decision, but I knew it was where God was calling me to go, and from it things like this book have come to life.

To everyone at Morgan James Publishing, thank you for all your help in making my dreams come true. It has been such a joy to work with all of you and watch this book come to life. I am eternally grateful that you all were willing to invest in me and make this book become something greater than I ever could have imagined on the day when I first sat down to write.

Last but certainly not least, thanks be to God. He is always faithful and will never call us to things without being there with us every step of the way. He saw things in me way before I ever saw them in myself, and this book would have never been possible without his grace, strength, and guidance along the way.

# Introduction

prayed to receive God into my life at an early age—I know, that's likely what you expect a Christian author to say, and knowing that may even give you the impression that I had my life together sooner than most. In reality, I made that prayer because I was both desperate and tired of suffering. I lived for years with the constant fear that I was alone. One day, I was told by someone that we are never alone because God is always present. I decided to find out if this presence was true, and asked God that if he was there with me, to take away my fear. Without fail, God took away my fear that same night. I knew he was real, but I would remain blind to just how much God cares about me for years.

I had this desire to be intimately *known*, and I needed answers. I knew what I wanted, but I didn't know how to find another person who shared that desire. Determined that I could find what I was looking for, I went on a search. Once I graduated high school and left home, my search and need to be known grew deeper. I distanced myself from the impersonal God I grew up with, and instead, I began to seek out a life of partying. Because I didn't know what my true identity was at the time, getting drunk made it "easier" to talk to people. The problem was that unless I was in a drunken state, most of those people lost their interest in me. Out of my own desperation to stay relevant, I continued further down the path of drinking.

My search ended one night when I was raped. In an instant, I went from searching for a way to be known, to feeling like no one would ever desire to get to know me again. On the outside, everything looked normal. I looked normal. On the inside, I felt disgusting and screamed to get out of my own body. I called out God's name for the first time in years. I couldn't believe he would let something like this happen to me. What did I do to deserve this?

I never knew the importance of an involvement in a community of women until the rape happened and it was seemingly "too late" to find one. I numbed my pain by drinking more excessively because it was the only way I knew how to distract myself from my own disgust. Until, a girl I had recently met asked me to go to church with her. Living in a state of rock bottom and seeing the fact that someone was willing to invest time in me, I figured I had nothing to lose and so I went. From this friendship, I was reintroduced to the Bible and began to see myself in a new, true light—a light that gave freedom and led me to the relationship I wanted all along—a relationship with God.

Now, I know where truth is found and I am confident in the person God made me to be. My "tell it like it is" personality allows me to weed out the lies Satan likes to tell us and send them back to where they came from by the power of the Holy Spirit. My desire is for each of you to live in the freedom that is found from knowing the truth of who you are and the truth of the one who made you.

Who were we made to be? Our identity? Our reason for being on this earth? We all have one. We all desire at some point in life to know our purpose. For any invention, innovation, or formula created, no one knows more about the purpose for creating them than their creator. In the case of every human being on this earth, that Creator is God. God wants each of us to get to know him on an intimate level. In doing so, we can also get to know ourselves.

> *"The God who made the world and everything in it is the Lord of heaven and earth and does not live in temples built by human hands. And he is not served by human hands, as if he needed anything. Rather, he himself gives everyone life and breath and everything else. From one man he made all the nations, that they should inhabit the whole earth; and he marked out their appointed times in history and the boundaries of their lands. God did this so that they would seek him and perhaps reach out for him and find him, though he is not far from any one of us."*
> Acts 17:24-27 NIV

In my own effort to seek and find God, he opened a door in my heart and gave me a very specific message to communicate. My hope is that this book provides a light to you and helps you learn and discover your true self. God made each of us the way we are for a specific purpose. He desires nothing more than to have a relationship with every single person on this earth in order to show us that purpose and the path for our lives.

> *Trust in the LORD with all your heart and lean not on your own*
> *understanding; in all your ways submit to him, and he will make*
> *your paths straight. Proverbs 3:5-6 NIV*

The world today surrounds us with distractions and tries to lead us away from the path God has for us. Some would say the world is a really dark place. Although darkness exists, God promises to all those who follow him that they will have the light of life.

> *When Jesus spoke again to the people, he said, "I am the light of*
> *the world. Whoever follows me will never walk in darkness, but*
> *will have the light of life." John 8:12 NIV*

When we have the light of life, darkness has no power over us. This means that Satan, being darkness, has no power over us when we are in God's light. He has no choice but to run away.

> *Submit yourselves, then, to God. Resist the devil, and he will flee*
> *from you. James 4:7 NIV*

Once we know the truth about who we are, we can live in freedom—the kind of freedom which can only be found in God and his truth.

> *So Jesus said to the Jews who had believed in him, "If you abide*
> *in my word, you are truly my disciples, and you will know the*
> *truth, and the truth will set you free." John 8:31-32 ESV*

It is important to note that God's truth *sets* us free. We have been freed from the bondage our sin creates. When we accept the punishment Jesus took on the cross for our sins, we are freed from that bondage. With this freedom, we are able to live out the life for which God has created us. Through Christ, we all have the strength and ability to love one another in the same way that God loves us. Freedom is a calling we each have on our lives.

> *You, my brothers and sisters, were called to be free. But do not*
> *use your freedom to indulge the flesh; rather, serve one another*
> *humbly in love. For the entire law is fulfilled in keeping this*
> *one command: "Love your neighbor as yourself." Galatians*
> *5:13-14 NIV*

However, as long as we live on this earth, various lies will be said to us. Lying is the language of the enemy. As described by Jesus in the book of John:

*"You belong to your father, the devil, and you want to carry out your father's desires. He was a murderer from the beginning, not holding to the truth, for there is no truth in him. When he lies, he speaks his native language, for he is a liar and the father of lies." John 8:44 NIV*

Although it is true that Satan will attempt to feed us lies for as long as we are on this earth, we do not have to believe them. Through God's power we are able to overcome all of the lies thrown our way.

*Finally, be strong in the Lord and in his mighty power. Put on the full armor of God, so that you can take your stand against the devil's schemes. Ephesians 6:10-11 NIV*

Part of that armor of God we are told to put on in order to fight against the devil's schemes consists of knowing the truth.

*Therefore put on the full armor of God, so that when the day of evil comes, you may be able to stand your ground, and after you have done everything, to stand. Stand firm then, with the belt of truth buckled around your waist, with the breastplate of righteousness in place, and with your feet fitted with the readiness that comes from the gospel of peace. In addition to all this, take up the shield of faith, with which you can extinguish all the flaming arrows of the evil one. Take the helmet of salvation and the sword of the Spirit, which is the word of God. Ephesians 6:13-17 NIV*

Just as the Bible warns us about the enemy being the father of lies, we are also told where the source of truth comes from.

*Jesus answered, "I am the way and the truth and the life. No one comes to the Father except through me." John 14:6 NIV*

Living in the fullness of who we were made to be consists of placing our faith in Jesus who is the way to true life. When we accept Jesus's punishment for our sins, we receive God's Holy Spirit, allowing us to form a relationship with God. A relationship with God is the *most important* relationship we can ever invest in. No one wants to spend time with us more than he does, and no one sees us in the same light as he does.

My prayer for everyone who reads this book is that it would be a tool in shedding God's light into all areas of your life. I pray that as a result of that light, you would be able to see yourselves in ways you have never seen yourself before, and that you would see yourselves in the same way God sees you.

I pray for freedom and truth to shine in any areas of your life currently being ruled by lies, and for the truths about God to be revealed to you—truths about his love for you and how much he cares about you. May this book bring you a renewed vision in the way you view your reason for being on this earth and in the way you view the one who brought you here.

# CHAPTER ONE
# I Am Interesting

## Lesson 1: Paying Attention

Being asked what interests us is a fundamental and go-to question many people resort to when first getting to know someone. On a materialistic level, this question is likely extremely easy for almost everyone to answer. It could be any sport, hobby, or craft. We all have things of interest we devote our free time to. However, what if we switched the wording of the question "What are your interests?" to "What makes you interesting?" Chances are, that second question is much more difficult or even uncomfortable to answer. But why? The truth "I am interesting" is necessary to have as a foundation to building one of the things God is interested in most: relationships. Most of us don't walk around saying how interesting we are, but the belief of this truth impacts both the way we view ourselves and how we view others dramatically.

Thinking about my own life, the struggle to believe this truth began at an early age. Most of the people who met me after high school would have a hard time believing this, but I was by far one of the quietest kids in my class for all of my childhood. I grew up with the mindset that, the more people knew about me, the more evidence they had to form false perceptions or stereotypes about me. My fear was largely the result of an insecurity about my own identity. I wanted close relationships with people, but I wasn't confident enough to share my personal story with them to get there. I knew I was more than a stereotype, and if people were actually interested in getting to know me further, they would have learned that too.

How do we believe the truth "I am interesting?"

**Interest:** *noun* curiosity, concern; *verb* to engage the attention of[1]

How do we engage the attention of something? One of the avenues leading to the belief of feeling interesting is through the belief that we can engage the attention of people, or that they want to pay their attention toward us. What makes arriving at this belief so hard?

To address this, we look to the fact that the phrase "paying attention" specifically includes the word *paying* in it. This indicates that in order for someone to focus their attention on or toward us, it *costs* them something. In my case, the cost was spending the time with me and them getting to know my true self.

Regardless of the cost's nature, when we struggle to see our worth, chances are we also struggle to see how someone else could want to pay their attention toward us.

**What do you find yourself paying attention to?**

_____

_____

_____

_____

**Can you think of any instances where you felt unworthy of someone's attention?**

_____

_____

_____

_____

---

1    *Merriam-Webster's Dictionary and Thesaurus,* Updated Edition, s.v. "Interest."

The truth is, God sees each of us as being worth the cost of his son's life. He is extremely interested in our well-being and desires each of us to pay attention to the things he has for us. What exactly should our attention be placed in?

> **God's Word**: *"Pay attention to all that I have said to you, and make no mention of the names of other gods, nor let it be heard on your lips." Exodus 23:13 ESV*
>
> **God's Commands**: *The LORD will make you the head, not the tail. If you pay attention to the commands of the LORD your God that I give you this day and carefully follow them, you will always be at the top, never at the bottom. Deuteronomy 28:13 NIV*
>
> **The Hearts of Others**: *But the LORD said to him, "Pay no attention to how tall and handsome he is. I have rejected him, because I do not judge as people judge. They look at the outward appearance, but I look at the heart." 1 Samuel 16:7*

As these verses suggest, our attention is to be put in things which cannot be seen by the human eye. Placing our attention in things unseen requires a greater level of interest and investment. Wherever our interests lie, our attention lies also. Our attention holds extreme value. The enemy also recognizes the value of our attention, so much so, that he tries to steal our attention constantly.

**How often do you find yourself becoming distracted from the things you should pay attention to? What draws your attention away during those times?**

_____

_____

_____

_____

We don't pay attention to things because we have to, but because we made the choice to. Having a physical presence and actually paying attention are vastly different.

When we successfully identify that people pay attention to us because they take interest in what we're saying or doing, believing the truth of "I am interesting" becomes much easier.

**How can you be more intentional in the ways you pay attention to others so that they know you show interest in them?**

_____

_____

_____

_____

**Do you ever struggle to feel that God is paying attention to you? If so, why?**

_____

_____

_____

_____

**How might you be able to pray into that situation and ask God to show you the attention he has for you?**

_____

_____

_____

_____

## Lesson 2: Curiosity

Since the dawn of our creation, curiosity has been a part of human nature. Dating back to the first sin committed by Eve in the garden, Satan fed into Eve's curiosity of the forbidden fruit and enticed her to take the bite. Just as Eve had a curiosity about the forbidden fruit, we each have different subjects of curiosity. Our curiosities lead to either good or sinful results dependent upon how we act on them.

Having five older siblings, I was always curious to know what their lives were like. Often times when they entertained my company, it included sports and video games. Let me tell you, no other elementary school-aged girl at that time knew more about basketball in the Michael Jordan era than I did. I got pretty good at playing basketball on video games too.

Our curiosity leads to a variety of both good and bad outcomes. Eve's curiosity was one of the variables that led to the first committed sin, but Isaac Newton also discovered gravity due to his curiosity of seeing an apple fall from a tree.

In another definition of "interest" we see the word "curiosity."[2] How does this concept of curiosity connect to where we place our interests?

**Curious:** *adjective* having a desire to investigate and learn[3]

When anyone possesses a desire to learn or know more about us, it's because we've piqued a curiosity in them. They are *interested* in us. This concept of piquing the curiosity of others was a contributing factor of my inability to see the truth that I am an interesting person. I often thought to myself, "Someone couldn't actually be curious enough about the little they knew about me to want to learn more, right?" There is no definite truth in that statement, but that's exactly what the enemy wanted me to believe, and I did. Believing this, I shielded others away from being able to get to know more about me. For the entirety of my childhood, shielding people away didn't seem like a big deal. I didn't need to have the skill of opening up to people because God blessed me with many great friends very early on in life. I kept the same five closest friends I had in first grade all the way through graduating high school. Aside from those friends, I prevented myself from forming newer potentially great and sustaining relationships.

---

2    *Merriam-Webster's Dictionary and Thesaurus,* Updated Edition, s.v. "Interest."
3    *Merriam-Webster's Dictionary and Thesaurus,* Updated Edition, s.v. "Curious."

When on the level of others wanting to get to know more about us, this concept of curiosity is somewhat easy to grasp. But, what if we instead internalize the focus and look at curiosity in the sense of us wanting to get to know ourselves better? Is it possible for someone to know us better than we know ourselves?

**Have you ever had the desire to learn or know more about yourself? Why or why not?**

_____

_____

_____

_____

There is someone who knows more about us than we know about ourselves, and that "someone" is God. He holds the ability to teach us about ourselves.
> *Your knowledge of me is too deep; it is beyond my understanding. Psalm 139:6*

**Have you ever asked God to teach you more about yourself? If so, when was the last time and what did that look like? If not, what are you curious to learn about yourself?**

_____

_____

_____

_____

At its root, our curiosity stems from a desire of some kind. In the Bible, we see two different types of desires. The desires of mankind and the desires of God. Ideally, our desires align with God's, but that's not always the case. How do we distinguish between the two? The Bible says that human desires:

**Give way to sin:** *But we are tempted when we are drawn away and trapped by our own evil desires. Then our evil desires conceive and give birth to sin; and sin, when it is full-grown, gives birth to death. James 1:14-15*

**Perpetuate ignorance:** *Therefore, with minds that are alert and fully sober, set your hope on the grace to be brought to you when Jesus Christ is revealed at his coming. As obedient children, do not conform to the evil desires you had when you lived in ignorance. But just as he who called you is holy, so be holy in all you do; 1 Peter 1:13-15 NIV*

Those verses bring us back to the first sin committed by Eve. The serpent in the garden tapped into Eve's curiosity of the forbidden fruit. Through her human desire of wanting to learn more about the knowledge of good and evil, she ate the fruit, committed the first sin, and the separation of God and mankind took place.

God's desires, unlike our own, are always free of unhealthy intentions. Another term used in the Bible when talking about the desires God has for us is "God's will." God has a will for each of us, what does his will consist of?

*For this is the will of God, that by doing good you should put to silence the ignorance of foolish people. Live as people who are free, not using your freedom as a cover-up for evil, but living as servants of God. 1 Peter 2:15-16 ESV*

Simply put, God wants us to live in freedom. In order to do so, we must devote our lives to him and have a relationship with him. If we don't, we are subject to become weighed down by the slavery to our own sin.

**Do you have a hard time aligning your desires to God's will for your life? What gets in the way for you to live a life of freedom?**

---------------------------------------------------------------

---------------------------------------------------------------

---------------------------------------------------------------

---------------------------------------------------------------

**What steps can you take to align your desires to God's will for your life to achieve freedom?**

_____

_____

_____

_____

~~~~~~~

## Lesson 3: Concern

If someone were to come to us and say they were concerned about us, many of us would likely go into a defensive mode. If we didn't know what they were referring to, we may even get concerned about them. Most often when we hear the word concern, we associate a negative connotation with it. Rightfully so, since one of the synonyms for "concern" is "worry."[4] But, for the purpose of this chapter, we are going to shift that focus. Worrying is *not* a characteristic of God. Instead, we will focus on the other aspect of the word, which is:

**Concern:** *verb* to relate to: be about [5]

**What things do you show concern for because of your close relation or connection to them?**

_____

_____

_____

_____

---

4    *Merriam-Webster's Dictionary and Thesaurus,* Updated Edition, s.v. "Concern."
5    *Merriam-Webster's Dictionary and Thesaurus,* Updated Edition, s.v. "Concern."

When it came to developing relationships in my childhood, concern was often the point where I stopped allowing people to enter my life. Externally, there was little evidence of anyone needing to be concerned for me. I had good grades, loving parents, and a group of a few good friends I was inseparable from. My house was the place to be after school. We had a swing set, trampoline, basketball hoop, and always had the best snacks to choose from.

To show the part of my life worthy of concern, I would need to open up about who I was internally. Because I seldom told people about my inner self, I gave them little to relate or connect with on a deeper level. Did people actually not want to relate with me? Of course not. It was my own assumption that someone would not be interested in getting to know me. Very little concern was necessary to be shown in making the friends I had growing up. All of them either lived in my neighborhood or had the same teachers in school, and they were the ones who asked me to be friends, not vice versa.

The truth is, there are a lot of people in this world interested in getting to know each one of us. When someone has an interest in us, showing concern for us comes as a result. Showing concern to others is of so much importance, that the Bible calls everyone in the body of Christ to show concern for one another.

> *...so that there should be no division in the body, but that its parts should have equal concern for each other. If one part suffers, every part suffers with it; if one part is honored, every part rejoices with it. 1 Corinthians 12:25-26 NIV*

Community is God's design. When we relate to and connect with other people, those people will develop a concern for us over time. They become *interested* in us. If we don't do our part in communicating who we really are to one another, we leave them nothing to connect with or take interest in. Chances are, most of us have more people who want to connect with us in our lives than we are aware of.

In order to recognize when others show concern for us, we must know what it looks like to show concern. What tools can we use to display a concern for one another?

> **Communicate their value:** *Therefore if you have any encouragement from being united with Christ, if any comfort from his love, if any common sharing in the Spirit, if any tenderness and compassion, then make my joy complete by being like-minded, having the same love, being one in spirit and of one mind. Do nothing out of selfish ambition or vain conceit.*

*Rather, in humility value others above yourselves, not looking to your own interests but each of you to the interests of the others. Philippians 2:1-4 NIV*

**Show justice:** *The righteous care about justice for the poor, but the wicked have no such concern. Proverbs 29:7 NIV*

**Share Jesus's interests:** *I hope in the Lord Jesus to send Timothy to you soon, that I also may be cheered when I receive news about you. I have no one else like him, who will show genuine concern for your welfare. For everyone looks out for their own interests, not those of Jesus Christ. Philippians 2:19-21 NIV*

**How can you become more like these verses and show value, justice, or interest to those around you?**

_____

_____

_____

_____

**How have other people done those things for you?**

_____

_____

_____

_____

Odds are, anyone who was behind those actions in the answer to the previous question finds interest in us.

We must be able to identify ways we relate and connect with other people as well as recognize the ways people build us up. Once both of those things happen, relationships we begin to form with others will develop a greater level of authenticity. Feeling uninteresting can be conquered when we experience authenticity in relationships. If the concept of relating to other people sounds daunting, start with relating to God. He desires nothing more than to have a relationship with everyone, and will never grow disinterested in pursing that relationship.

*But God demonstrates his own love for us in this: While we were*
*still sinners, Christ died for us. Romans 5:8 NIV*

God's concern for having a relationship with us is so great, his only son Jesus died for our salvation even during the midst of our sin. Nothing can ever take away God's interest in us—all we have to do is invite him into our lives.

**What areas do you find yourself struggling to relate with others?**

_____

_____

_____

_____

**How can you invite God into those areas and allow him to show you how he finds interest in you?**

_____

_____

_____

_____

## Lesson 4: Involvement

I would first like for us all to take a moment and think about the last time we sat in church and heard our pastor say, "We don't know what to with all of the people wanting to get involved." The answer to that question for almost every one of us is likely "Never." There is no shortage of work to be done in the church:

> *Then he said to his disciples, "The harvest is plentiful, but the laborers are few; therefore pray earnestly to the Lord of the harvest to send out laborers into his harvest." Matthew 9:37-38 ESV*

Ideally, the activities we choose to be involved in are a product of where our interests lie. Part of believing the truth "I am interesting" means believing our interests have merit. A good portion of my involvement all throughout my childhood included the involvement around sharing in other people's interests rather than my own. I didn't always do this out of the bottom of my heart as a good friend, but rather to avoid the potential disappointment I would have felt if they didn't want to be involved with activities that surrounded my interests. Let's be honest, I spent another good portion of my time as a kid at home practicing flash cards and playing math-based computer games. Who would want to know about the latest problem I learned how to solve?

We frequently put the interests God has given us on the back-burner because we fail to see the use or benefit of them. Other times, we simply disregard our interests because we've already invested too much time elsewhere. On the surface, having investments in many areas is not always a bad thing, but it has the potential to become one when we neglect the calling God has for each of our lives because don't have the time to live out our calling.

**What are some of the people, places, or organizations with which you are currently involved?**

_____

_____

_____

_____

**Why did you choose to be involved with each of them, and how is God glorified in them?**

_____

_____

_____

_____

Just as the church needs involvement from its members to succeed, we need people to be involved in our lives. When Jesus refers to the "harvest" in the passage from Matthew, he is referring to *us*. People.

Anytime we become involved in something, it requires some level of commitment from us. Commitment takes on multiple different forms. As followers of Christ, we must be committed to putting in the work required to cultivate the plentiful harvest that awaits. Our commitment comes in these forms:

> **Work**: *Commit your work to the LORD, and your plans will be established. Proverbs 16:3 ESV*
>
> **Trust**: *Trust in the LORD with all your heart and lean not on your own understanding; in all your ways submit to him, and he will make your paths straight. Proverbs 3:5-6 NIV*
>
> **Faith**: *By faith Abraham, when called to go to a place he would later receive as his inheritance, obeyed and went, even though he did not know where he was going. By faith he made his home in the promised land like a stranger in a foreign country; he lived in tents, as did Isaac and Jacob, who were heirs with him of the same promise. For he was looking forward to the city with foundations, whose architect and builder is God. Hebrews 11:8-10 NIV*
>
> **Finances**: *"For where your treasure is, there your heart will be also." Matthew 6:21 ESV*

**What do these verses indicate as being some of the results of placing our commitment to God?**

_____

_____

_____

_____

**What stops you from further committing or involving yourself with God?**

_____

_____

_____

_____

**Think back to times in your life where people were committed to you or engaged in you in some way. Who were they and what did they do?**

_____

_____

_____

_____

Chances are, the people listed in the above questions find interest in us. To cultivate healthy relationships, we must be willing to both be involved in people's lives and receive the involvement of other people into our life. Not doing so could unintentionally communicate to the other person that we are disinterested in them.

**How can you display commitment to your everyday relationships, so that those close to you see your interest in them?**

_____

_____

_____

_____

## Lesson 5: Boredom

Have you ever had someone tell you they find watching paint dry to be an interesting activity? I would bet that none of us have, as the phrase "it's like watching paint dry" is used as a metaphor to represent boredom. The word "boring" is an antonym to the word "interesting."[6] Meaning, if we have a hard time believing the truth "I am interesting," chances are we also struggle with believing the truth "I am not boring."

These two truths sound drastically different. One tells us something that we *are* and the other tells us something that we *aren't*, but at their core, they are the same. Leading into this last lesson of the "I am interesting" chapter. What does boredom look like?

**Boredom:** *noun* the condition of being weary and restless
because of dullness [7]

Upon researching the topic for this lesson, I found no references on where the Bible describes a person to be dull or boring. God created each and every one of us as reflections of him. If he isn't boring, he didn't create us as boring either.

However, I did find instances in the Bible where it describes people as *becoming* dull. Indicating, this "dullness" isn't a characteristic of the people themselves, but rather a *product* of the choices or actions they made. What does dullness look like?

---

6    *Merriam-Webster's Dictionary and Thesaurus*, Updated Edition, s.v. "Interesting."
7    *Merriam-Webster's Dictionary and Thesaurus*, Updated Edition, s.v. "Boredom."

*About this we have much to say, and it is hard to explain, since you have become dull of hearing. For though by this time you ought to be teachers, you need someone to teach you again the basic principles of the oracles of God. You need milk, not solid food, for everyone who lives on milk is unskilled in the word of righteousness, since he is a child. But solid food is for the mature, for those who have their powers of discernment trained by constant practice to distinguish good from evil. Hebrews 5:11-14 ESV*

**Can you think of a time where you were dull of hearing? What was the result of that situation?**

_____

_____

_____

_____

**Can you think of a time where you exhibited discernment? What was the result of that situation?**

_____

_____

_____

_____

Those verses point out that they were dull to hearing, or in other words, they were *uninterested* in hearing. The people being addressed were intended to be something more or greater than their current state. They were intended to be teachers, but because of their lack of hearing, they instead needed to be taught.

The good news is, every single one of us has been given a power of discernment. The choice lies with us to receive and exercise powers of discernment or not. Dullness is a *choice*—not something we have to carry around with us. If we use our powers of discernment, we gain the maturity necessary to handle greater things than those who do not choose to exercise them. The lack of exercise in those powers leads to the dullness of hearing.

That same concept can be applied when evaluating our relationships with others—we allow our perception of boredom to limit our greatness. For much of my childhood, I shied away from approaching people because I didn't see how anyone would be interested in getting to know me. For that reason, one of my best friendships was made as a result of her approaching me. I stood at the edge of the playground away from the traffic of people one recess during elementary school, when a girl came up and asked me if I wanted to play with her. I tended to keep quiet and to myself during school, unwilling to risk the hurt of someone not wanting to get to know me. However, when she broke that initial barrier for me, I said "yes" and gained a great life-long friend as a result.

Although that interaction had a profound impact on my life, I felt in general that I did people a favor by relieving them of potential boredom from having to listen to what I had to say. Discerning this concept on a deeper level, believing someone won't want to hear what I have to say contains an unfair assumption about the other person. How can I know others' true interest in me before even attempting to form a relationship with them? I can't.

We can each rest assured that we were each created by a God who is mindful of details. God never grows bored of hearing from us, and if we ever find ourselves becoming dull of hearing, we can lay those feelings down at the cross. Dullness is not something we have to own. God is extremely interested in every single one of us.

**What are some things that lead you to feeling like you're a dull or boring person?**

_____

_____

_____

_____

**How might we open our ears to use our powers of discernment to help both ourselves and others overcome this lie that we are boring?**

_____

_____

_____

_____

Dear God,

I ask that you would reveal to me the areas in my life in which I should be paying both more and less attention to. Help me to show an interest in others in the same way that you show interest in me. Teach me something new about myself that will help me to see how my human desires lead to sin. Replace those desires with a hunger to know more about your will for my life. I confess that most of the time I am more concerned about myself than I am other people, and that I don't do enough to recognize and acknowledge other people's concern for me. Supply me with the strength to be more committed to you in my actions, trust, faith, finances, and relationships. Open my ears to hear all of the ways in which you find me interesting, so that I may also combat the lie that I am boring.

In Jesus' name,
Amen.

## CHAPTER TWO
# I Am Creative

### Lesson 1: Power

What is the first thing that comes to mind when thinking about the word "power?" My first thought was the phrase "I've got the power." With that phrase in mind, I want to spend the rest of the lesson talking about the truth it holds. Each and every person who follows God has access to his power, including the power to create. What does it mean to be creative?

**Creative:** *adjective* marked by the ability or power to create[8]

Growing up, the characteristic I was most known for in school was my math ability. I taught myself math at an early age, gaining endless hours of practice with basic math by playing Yahtzee around the dinner table with family. I flew through grade school math and broke school records with the depth of my multiplication knowledge. My dominance even got to the point where teachers would ask if I wanted sit out of the math games we played in class to give other kids a chance to win.

Someone back then could have easily convinced me that I was the best mathematician in the school. What they couldn't have convinced me of was my ability to create. So I did 9 times 7 faster than everyone else, big deal. We would all reach the same answer eventually.

We are all highly creative in our own way. One of my ways was visualizing math problems in my head and solving them in a quick and accurate manner. My creativity allows me to approach math problems in ways many people shy

---

8    *Merriam-Webster's Dictionary and Thesaurus,* Updated Edition, s.v. "Creative."

away from because dealing with complex or large quantities of numbers can be intimidating.

**Have you ever found yourself believing that you're not a creative person? If so, what are some things that have kept you from believing that?**

_____

_____

_____

_____

The ability to create is a characteristic. In other words, things don't create themselves. The only one who has the ability to create something out of nothing is God.

> In the beginning God created the heavens and the earth. Genesis 1:1 NIV

Looking at the definition of creative we see that something that is creative has the "power to create."[9] Just because the enemy doesn't possess as much power as God, doesn't mean that he isn't powerful. The powers he does possess, however, are far from original. Satan uses the same tactics to tempt us today that he used with Adam and Eve. Satan is aware of his defeat as a result of Jesus's death on the cross, but he will continue to use the same tactics to take as many people with him until the day heaven and earth are restored. When we become aware of the enemy's nature, it allows us to call him out on his schemes. Some of those schemes are:

> **Craftiness:** Now the serpent was more crafty than any other beast of the field that the LORD God had made. Genesis 3:1 ESV
> **Disguise:** And no wonder, for even Satan disguises himself as an angel of light. 2 Corinthians 11:14 ESV
> **Theft:** "The thief comes only to steal and kill and destroy; I have come that they may have life, and have it to the full." John 10:10 NIV

---

9    Merriam-Webster's Dictionary and Thesaurus, Updated Edition, s.v. "Creative."

**In what ways has the enemy used these tactics in your life? How have you been able to overcome them?**

_____

_____

_____

_____

By being made in the image of God, the Creator himself, we can possess the power to overcome any of the enemy's schemes at any time.

*So God created mankind in his own image, in the image of God he created them; male and female he created them. Genesis 1:27 NIV*

God created each of us in his image. When we accept his Holy Spirit into our lives, we have access to his power. However, our reason for creation and what work that consists of looks different for each of us. Although each of us was created for a different reason, those reasons all serve one common purpose.

*Whatever you do, work at it with all your heart, as working for the Lord, not for human masters, Colossians 3:23 NIV*

God uses us as his co-laborers here on earth. Everything we do should be done in the spirit of working for him.

**What types of works has God created for you to do?**

_____

_____

_____

_____

**What qualities has he blessed you with to do those works?**

_____

_____

_____

_____

**How can you take those qualities and recognize the power they have in creating good for God's kingdom?**

_____

_____

_____

_____

〜〜〜〜

## Lesson 2: Thoughts

When people find out someone we know is going through a rough time, one of the first phrases we say to them is "I will keep you in my thoughts and prayers." Why is that? Often, it is said out of reflex and assuming it is the right thing to say. The reality is, our thoughts contain power—power capable of bringing peace, restoration, and glorification. Putting our thoughts into some form of expression is the very essence of all mediums of art. Be it drawing, singing, dancing, etc., any time we see or hear an "original" piece of artwork, we associate creativity with the person behind it. Rightfully so, because each one of them _is_ highly creative.

In any form, our creativity originates from our thoughts. Creativity in the form of expression is simply putting into motion an idea that came to us in some form of thought. Part of believing the truth "I am creative" involves recognizing the originality or uniqueness in our thoughts.

I spent most of my early years in silence. I kept my thoughts to myself unless I could see what product would come from them. Instead of asking people to help me learn things I didn't understand, I preferred figuring them out on my own. In elementary school, I taught myself how to roller skate. It took a lot of going back and forth on the dead-end street we lived on to get it right, but after a few falls and some bruises to go along with them, I mastered the science behind the transfer of weight.

My preference to figure things out for myself could have come as a product of being the youngest child of six—there was nothing I saw someone else do that I didn't also think I could figure out for myself. With my problem-solving abilities, I often found a sufficient answer. However, doing so prevented me from experiencing the net gain of both learning from other people and sharing my skills with them.

None of us were created to live on this earth and only keep our thoughts to ourselves. We are the only human on this planet who knows our thoughts, giving Satan all the more reason to scare us into keeping our thoughts silent.

**How often do you find yourself holding your thoughts back because you feel that what you are thinking will not result in and value add or creative dimension to the conversation at hand?**

_____

_____

_____

_____

We hinder ourselves from seeing the creativity in our thoughts when we view creativity in the form of a *product* rather than a *process*. The word "create" is a verb,[10] an action. The product formed from the act of creating is a creation. In reality, any creation we've ever seen or heard involved many intricate thoughts put into it by the creator during the process of form- ing the creation.

---

10   *Merriam-Webster's Dictionary and Thesaurus,* Updated Edition, s.v. "Create."

How much power do our thoughts have? Other than God, we are the only person who knows our thoughts. Let us all pause for a moment and let that sink in. Satan is incapable of knowing our thoughts. He is not omniscient.

> "...then hear from heaven, your dwelling place. Forgive and act; deal with everyone according to all they do, since you know their hearts (for you alone know every human heart)," 1 Kings 8:39 NIV

> For who knows a person's thoughts except the spirit of that person, which is in him? So also no one comprehends the thoughts of God except the Spirit of God. Now we have received not the spirit of the world, but the Spirit who is from God, that we might understand the things freely given us by God. 1 Corinthians 2:11-12 ESV

**Do you understand the things God has freely given you? Why or why not?**

_____

_____

_____

_____

From these verses we see the power our thoughts contain. God and our own self are the only ones who have access to them. Our thoughts allow us to understand the Spirit and the things God freely gives to us. The enemy has an extreme disadvantage from this lack of knowledge. Because of this, Satan will do anything he can to affect our surroundings in an attempt to influence our thoughts. He has seen humans interacting for thousands of years and has gathered enough data to predict very accurately our tendencies in situations.

Through the power of God, we are able to conquer Satan's attempts to influence our thoughts.

> Finally, be strong in the Lord and in his mighty power. Put on the full armor of God, so that you can take your stand against the devil's schemes. For our struggle is not against flesh and blood, but against the rulers, against the authorities, against the

*powers of this dark world and against the spiritual forces of evil in the heavenly realms. Ephesians 6:10-12 NIV*

When we value and recognize the power our thoughts have, the enemy's power loses its effect. Using the armor of God, we have the ability to defeat the enemy at all times. How can we use God's power to make sure we are taking full advantage of wearing the armor of God? Continuing on in Ephesians 6, it describes each piece in the suit of armor.

*Stand firm then, with the belt of truth buckled around your waist, with the breastplate of righteousness in place, and with your feet fitted with the readiness that comes from the gospel of peace. In addition to all this, take up the shield of faith, with which you can extinguish all the flaming arrows of the evil one. Take the helmet of salvation and the sword of the Spirit, which is the word of God. Ephesians 6:14-17 NIV*

Notice how out of each piece of armor, the only one that is offensive in nature is the sword of the Spirit, emulated by the word of God. Any time Satan attempts to attack our thoughts, we can attack back using the word of God.

*For the word of God is alive and active. Sharper than any double-edged sword, it penetrates even to dividing soul and spirit, joints and marrow; it judges the thoughts and attitudes of the heart. Nothing in all creation is hidden from God's sight. Everything is uncovered and laid bare before the eyes of him to whom we must give account. Hebrews 4:12-13 NIV*

Not only is God's word a sword, it is the *sharpest* sword. Nothing beats or overtakes God's word, including Satan. If the thoughts in our mind don't align with the word of God, they are *not from God*—it is indeed that simple. God will never contradict himself or set us up for failure.

**How has God's word helped you attack back at any negative thoughts you've had?**

_____

_____

_____

_____

**Which piece of armor is hardest for you to put on and why?**

_____

_____

_____

_____

_____

**Which piece of armor is easiest for you to put on? How can you use your strength to encourage those around you to do the same?**

_____

_____

_____

_____

_____

## Lesson 3: Imaginations

How different would the world look if each of us acted on making the world look like the kind of place we imagine it could be? Thinking of *our imaginations* in the context of that question alone sheds light upon the power our imaginations hold.

The concept of being *imaginative,* or using our imaginations, is another form of creativity. In thinking about the last time that I heard someone compliment my own imagination, I would have to go back to childhood. Imagining was easier to come by then. During my childhood, I cruised around my neighborhood in my electrically-powered vehicle as if I were in a real car capable of exploring the world. I built structures that came to life the second I secured the last piece in its place. The best part? No one questioned the validity of my experiences in either case.

As an adult, things look different. More frequently than children, we look at situations from a realistic mindset rather than an imaginative mindset. In fact, our society often places a negative association to what having an imagination means once we reach adulthood. If someone were to tell us we have "quite the imagination" as an adult, they're likely calling us crazy or just dismissing our opinion completely. The truth is, what's even crazier than someone attempting to degrade us by saying we have "quite the imagination" is us believing them and in return degrading ourselves.

Now obviously, our imaginations don't disappear from us the day we turn eighteen. But it isn't surprising that we begin to disregard having an imagination as an adult since imaginations are often perceived in a child-like manner. This perception of imaginations containing high value in children is quite the opposite from the perception of thoughts. We often view adults as generating much more valuable thoughts than children. In either case, our thoughts and our imaginations both involve an aspect of the formation or creation of something. What differences exist between the two?

> **Thought:** *noun* an individual act or product of thinking: idea[11]
>
> **Imagination:** *noun* the act or power of forming a mental image of something not present to the senses or not previously known or experienced[12]

No matter our age, we all possess a unique perspective in our thoughts and imaginations, making each of us highly creative in a way unlike any other human. Obviously, children contain fewer experiences than adults, which is one explanation of why we perceive children to be more imaginative than adults. But is that perception true? I would argue that it isn't. How would our perceptions change if instead of looking at adults as having more or less of an imagination than children, we took the viewpoint that adults have the ability to imagine about much greater things than children because of their larger foundation of both knowledge and experiences? When we become so busy dismissing imaginations after a certain age, it stunts our ability to both continue to exercise our imagination and gain a greater ability to imagine.

---

11   *Merriam-Webster's Dictionary and Thesaurus,* Updated Edition, s.v. "Thought."
12   *Merriam-Webster's Dictionary and Thesaurus,* Updated Edition, s.v. "Imagination."

**Do you consider yourself to be an imaginative person? Why or why not?**

_____

_____

_____

Exactly how powerful is our imagination? We see in the definition of "imagination" that it is a "mental image."[13] Tying these concepts back to the previous lesson, if we know Satan is *incapable* of knowing our thoughts, and our imagination exists mentally or in our minds, this would imply he also can't read our imaginations. Although our imaginations are based off of things not seen or experienced, and many of the things we imagine will never be experiences we encounter in the future, that does not stop God from using our imagination to work in us. God gives many of us visions or images to help guide us along the path he has laid out for our lives. Just how much can God do with our imagination?

> *Now to him who is able to do immeasurably more than all we ask or imagine, according to his power that is at work within us, to him be glory in the church and in Christ Jesus throughout all generations, for ever and ever! Amen. Ephesians 3:20-21 NIV*

How much can he do? *Immeasurably* more than we ask or imagine. Discrediting our imaginations also discredits the amount of work God is capable of doing. So instead, I encourage everyone to imagine, and to imagine *big*. We serve a big God and he wants nothing more than to give us more than we even know how to ask for.

**Has God ever spoken to you through your imagination? If so, how and what did you do in response to the image presented to you?**

_____

_____

_____

---

13  *Merriam-Webster's Dictionary and Thesaurus,* Updated Edition, s.v. "Imagination."

**In the past, how has God given you more than you could ask or imagine?**

_____

_____

_____

_____

**Have you had any recent images given to you that you don't know how to respond to? How can we be a community of believers that encourages one another to explore and exercise our imaginations?**

_____

_____

_____

_____

~~~~~~~

## Lesson 4: Productivity

With the amount of distractions the world offers today, productivity has never been easier to ignore. Just because we are able to ignore productivity more easily than ever before, does not mean the world ignores the value of productivity. Our world *thrives* on productivity. Many of us at times even judge our own self-worth by our personal productivity. When I saw that the word "productive" is a synonym to the word "creative,"[14] I originally struggled to see the similarities between the two. That is, until I came to the realization that just like creativity, productivity is a process. Similar to how creations are the result of the process of creativity, products are the result of the process of productivity.

---

14 *Merriam-Webster's Dictionary and Thesaurus,* Updated Edition, s.v. "Creative."

During grade school, when it came to the subject of reading books, productivity was nowhere to be found for me. For almost all of 3rd–5th grades, I continually failed to produce the results my teachers wanted, and for it was held back at the same reading level for the majority of all three of those years. With teachers who were desperate to find solutions to my problem, they at one point took me out of class to see the school speech counselor to work on improving my language abilities. I would sit with the speech counselor in their office, go through some flashcards, and pass through the deck with flying colors. It didn't take long for my teacher to realize that type of help wasn't what I needed. I didn't need someone to teach me how to read—I learned how to read before I stepped foot into kindergarten. What I needed was coaching on how to produce their desired results.

**When was the last time you felt productive? What caused you to feel productive, and did you also feel creative in the process?**

_____

_____

_____

_____

**Why does what you produce matter?**

_____

_____

_____

_____

**Productive:** *adjective* having the quality or power of producing esp. in abundance[15]

15  *Merriam-Webster's Dictionary and Thesaurus,* Updated Edition, s.v. "Productive."

As the definition indicates, productivity contains *power*. The power of productivity is spoken of many times within the Bible, often in the context of producing either "good" or "bad" fruits. The products that are created as a result of those good and bad fruits vary greatly. In order to turn away from producing bad fruits and toward the good fruits God desires, we must first be aware of the attributes that go into producing each type.

Elements attributed to producing bad fruits are:

**Anger:** *My dear brothers and sisters, take note of this: Everyone should be quick to listen, slow to speak and slow to become angry, because human anger does not produce the righteousness that God desires. James 1:19-20 NIV*

**Foolishness:** *Don't have anything to do with foolish and stupid arguments, because you know they produce quarrels. 2 Timothy 2:23 NIV*

**Sin:** *But sin, seizing the opportunity afforded by the commandment, produced in me every kind of coveting. For apart from the law, sin was dead. Romans 7:8 NIV*

When we use our creativity in ways of anger, foolishness, or sin, it produces quarrels, coveting, and corruption.

**Recall a recent situation in which one of these things was present in your life, what was produced as a result of that situation?**

_____

_____

_____

_____

In contrast, the Bible also lays out for us elements that produce good fruits:

**Serving God:** *"Very truly I tell you, unless a kernel of wheat falls to the ground and dies, it remains only a single seed. But if it dies, it produces many seeds. Anyone who loves their life will lose it, while anyone who hates their life in this world will keep it for eternal life. Whoever serves me must follow me; and where*

*I am, my servant also will be. My Father will honor the one who serves me." John 12:24-26 NIV*

**<u>Discipline</u>:** *No discipline seems pleasant at the time, but painful. Later on, however, it produces a harvest of righteousness and peace for those who have been trained by it. Hebrews 12:11 NIV*

**<u>Being filled with the Spirit</u>:** *But the Spirit produces love, joy, peace, patience, kindness, goodness, faithfulness, humility, and self-control. There is no law against such things as these. And those who belong to Christ Jesus have put to death their human nature with all its passions and desires. The Spirit has given us life; he must also control our lives. Galatians 5:22-25*

Using our creativity in the areas of serving God, discipline, and being filled with the Spirit produces righteousness and eternal life.

**Can you recall a recent situation where the result of having one of the above qualities resulted in bearing good fruits? What were the good fruits produced?**

_____

_____

_____

_____

**What does allowing the Spirit to control your life tangibly look like to you?**

_____

_____

_____

_____

**What fears present in your life prevent you from allowing the Spirit to have control?**

_____

_____

_____

_____

Dear God,

I ask for you to shift the way I view the meaning of creativity. Help me to see how creativity is inherent to my nature of being your creation, and that creativity is a power. A power enabling me to think, imagine, and produce results paving the way for the work on this earth you have created me for. Provide me with the wisdom to recognize in what areas I may be holding back on utilizing my creativity. Reshape any areas where I feel like my thoughts don't have any value, especially when those thoughts relate to work drawing me closer to you. Show me where I struggle to put on your full armor. Reveal to me how to more boldly walk with the gospel of peace and the shield of faith. Teach me how to walk in my daily life wearing your armor confidently and not feeling weighed down. Guide my thoughts and my imagination in the direction of being honoring to you. Help me to discern any messages you may be attempting to communicate to me through my imagination. Thank you for being a God who produces nothing but good fruits. You are the perfect example I can refer to in order to produce good fruits in my own life. Show me how my anger, foolishness, or sin leads to the production of bad fruits. Replace them with a sense of discipline, a desire to serve you, and the fruits of your Spirit. Thank you for creating me and giving me the same power to create good things for your glory.

In Jesus' name,
Amen.

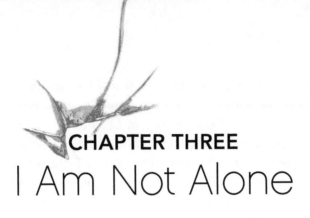

## CHAPTER THREE

# I Am Not Alone

## Lesson 1: Isolation

The truth "I am not alone" is a foundational concept to grasp in order to understand the very nature of God. Shortly after creating Adam in Genesis chapter 2, God states in verse 18, *"...It is not good for the man to be alone..."* *NIV* This statement led to the creation of Eve. Now, it would stand to reason that if God says it *is not* good for man to be alone, Satan would say it *is* good for man to be alone. The good news for us is that we are never alone—God is always present.

> *"The LORD himself goes before you and will be with you; he will never leave you nor forsake you. Do not be afraid; do not be discouraged." Deuteronomy 31:8 NIV*

In my own life, this concept took a while to grasp. I grew up with an extreme fear of being alone that only got worse as elementary school progressed into middle school. I had always been comfortable around people I had established relationships with, but being alone was a different story. I knew I had those few good friends I could hang out with during the day, but as soon as the sun went down, the street lights turned on, and we all went home from riding bikes around the neighborhood, the fear crept in. Night after night, I went to bed and laid there for hours trembling with fear. In an effort to quantify the phenomena my body would experience frequently, I gave these episodes a name and called them "shivers." During these shivers, I felt an all-encompassing negative presence and encountered nightmares regularly. A good night's sleep was a rare occurrence.

I had no solution for overcoming my fear if I stayed in my room alone. The spirit behind the negative presence was much more powerful than myself. Instead, I got myself out of my situation of isolation as soon as possible, ran to the next closest person, and clung to them for the assurance that I wasn't alone. This would cure my symptoms of fear for the night, but the scene would repeat multiple nights a week. What I really wanted was a relationship and closeness that no human is capable of providing in a constant manner. At this point in life, I had yet to put my faith in God. Church was just a place I went to on Sunday mornings out of family routine. As far as I was concerned, any time I laid in my room by myself, I was alone and powerless. The temporary alleviation of my fear was better than nothing.

Feeling alone encompasses many different identities. Whether in the context of feeling alone in not understanding a concept in a class we just attended, or feeling alone in living life with no one to turn to, we've all been in a similar place. That place of being afraid to speak up to someone or feeling like we have nowhere to go. Being blinded from the truth "I am not alone" is arguably one of the most powerful tactics the enemy uses on us.

**Alone:** *adjective* separated from others[16]

Digging further into this truth, we look to the story of Adam and Eve. As I've previously said, one of the first truths we read about in the Bible is how God created us to live in community with one another.

*Then the LORD God said, "It is not good for the man to live alone.*
*I will make a suitable companion to help him." Genesis 2:18*

Whenever we feel alone in our experiences, we often do the exact opposite of this verse and instead of being with someone, we isolate ourselves. We become afraid to ask for help or, in the case of my shivers, we ask for help in places that can only provide a temporary fix.

**Is there anything you are going through right now in which you are isolating yourself?**

_____

_____

_____

16   *Merriam-Webster's Dictionary and Thesaurus,* Updated Edition, s.v. "Alone."

Satan knows he has a far greater chance of getting us to both hear and believe the lies that he feeds us with when we isolate ourselves. The power of having people come together in the name of Jesus is far greater than any power he possesses. The following verses provide insight to the kind of power community provides.

> *Two are better than one, because they have a good return for their labor: If either of them falls down, one can help the other up. But pity anyone who falls and has no one to help them up. Also, if two lie down together, they will keep warm. But how can one keep warm alone? Though one may be overpowered, two can defend themselves. A cord of three strands is not quickly broken. Ecclesiastes 4:9-12 NIV*

> *"And I tell you more: whenever two of you on earth agree about anything you pray for, it will be done for you by my Father in heaven. For where two or three come together in my name, I am there with them." Matthew 18:19-20*

> *This is the message we have heard from him and declare to you: God is light; in him there is no darkness at all. 1 John 1:5 NIV*

Not only does community help us pick one another up, but the verses from Matthew promise us God's presence in any place where two or more gather in his name. If God's presence resides where two or more gather in his name, and if God is light and no darkness is in his presence, then Satan, being darkness, has absolutely no place to stay among a group of believers gathered together in the name of God. With that said, the *only* one who thrives when we isolate ourselves is the enemy himself. Let me say that again—Satan is the only one who thrives when we isolate ourselves.

Looking again into Genesis chapter 2, God spends the rest of the chapter creating a partner for Adam: Eve. The last verse of that chapter says, *Adam and his wife were both naked, and they felt no shame. Genesis 2:25 NIV* Afterward, the *very next verse* begins with the serpent tempting Eve in the garden. He catches Eve in a time where she is physically isolated from Adam and begins feeding her nothing but lies.

> *Now the snake was the most cunning animal that the LORD God had made. The snake asked the woman, "Did God really tell you not to eat fruit from any tree in the garden?" Genesis 3:1*

Like we see in the case of this verse, the lies Satan feeds us often come in the form of "half-truths." Satan knew what God told them. Did God tell them not to eat a fruit from the garden? Yes. Did God say not to eat fruit from *any* tree in the garden? No. God told Adam and Eve not to eat from one *specific* tree in the garden. However, when catching Eve alone, the serpent's question was close enough to the actual truth and she ate of the forbidden fruit.

When we isolate ourselves, we fall into the same types of traps as Eve. We begin to seek out our selfish human desires rather than God's desires. What does the Bible say about isolation?

*Whoever isolates himself seeks his own desire; he breaks out against all sound judgment. Proverbs 18:1 ESV*

Isolation and pursuing our own desires results in making decisions counter to those of a sound judgment. Only one perfectly sound judge exists: God.

**Do you ever find yourself falling into traps similar to the one set up by the serpent for Eve? How or in what way?**

_____

_____

_____

_____

_____

**How do the burdens you experience during trials you go through get lifted when bringing them to the surface in the form of prayer and in community?**

_____

_____

_____

_____

**How can you facilitate those kinds of relationships with people to be part of a community for others too?**

_____

_____

_____

_____

_____

~~~~~~

## Lesson 2: Separation

Numerous reasons exist as to why events of separation occur. We separate from other people if we feel they aren't healthy to associate with, we separate assets when needing to evenly distribute them to different people, and we separate territories by placing barriers around them. In each of the scenarios described, the separation forms two or more distinct divisions out of what was at one time together or unified. If we get to the point where we completely separate ourselves, we find ourselves in a place of solitude. We are alone.

In general, our society isn't very accepting of people creating division by excluding *others*. We all desire equal treatment. However, this isn't as much the case when we talk about us excluding *ourselves*. In fact, in our highly technology-based society, we even *crave* disconnection from time to time.

From a biblical standpoint, separation is representative of one main cause: sin. Often times, our craving for disconnection leads us to the committing of sins. We know sin is bad, but we do it anyway with the knowledge that it brings upon division of some sort, internally or externally. Reading that last sentence may sound silly at first, but what makes sinning so attractive? Sin has been attractive to every single one of us at some point, it's in our human nature. Why are we so quick to choose our way over God's?

The word sin is derived from a Greek word used as an archery term meaning "missing the mark." The "mark" in this case being the Law of the Old Testament. God knew no human upon exercising their own free will would successfully fulfill the Law. For this reason, he sent his son Jesus to be a ful-fillment of the Law. As a result of Jesus's fulfillment of the Law, we are able to fully embrace the truth that we are never alone.

Those of us who claim Christianity know our sin separates us from God, and yet we sin anyway. This looks different for each of us. For myself, it's often because my way is "easier" than God's way, or I just don't place complete trust in the fact God's way is better than my own. The most prominent example of this distrust during my childhood was with my epilepsy. As a baby, I was dropped on my head from about three feet up onto a cement floor, which frac-tured my skull and caused swelling. I was taken to the ER and had a CT scan done on my brain. The scan showed that there appeared to be nothing on the left side of my brain. Where there should have been brain tissue, it was black because of a fluid-filled cyst. Based on the scan, I later had a couple of brain surgeries to place a shunt to relieve the cyst. After the surgery, a second scan was done showing the surgery's success and that my brain was in its correct place. Thankfully, my ability to do basic functions like walk and talk formed. Being dropped and catching the cyst actually saved my life and has kept me on this earth today, but during this same time I was diagnosed with epilepsy.

While there is no sin I can commit to take away my epilepsy, not having epilepsy would certainly make my life "easier." Having epilepsy certainly doesn't make my life "better" either—not in any story I write.

Lending to one of the reasons why I now allow God to write my story. Unlike any of us, God uses all parts of our story for good. But what I find most interesting about this subject is, the only person truly who is alone when it comes to separation from our sins is God himself.

>  *It is because of your sins that he doesn't hear you. It is your sins that*
>  *separate you from God when you try to worship him. Isaiah 59:2*

When we sin, we separate ourselves from God. Jesus is the only human to walk this earth and live a life free of sin. As a result, he defeated death and the grave. Without Jesus, we all remain separated from God.

**Do you ever find yourself purposefully disconnecting from God? How or in what ways?**

_____

_____

_____

_____

**Do you ever feel a separation from God after acting out on a sin? How are those feelings exhibited?**

_____

_____

_____

_____

Aside from Jesus, the people in the Bible were not any less guilty of sin than we are today. Using the people in the Bible as an example, how can we expect to feel when we insist on doing things our way instead of God's way?

**Unworthy:** *"When he came to his senses, he said, 'How many of my father's hired servants have food to spare, and here I am starving to death! I will set out and go back to my father and say to him: Father, I have sinned against heaven and against you. I am no longer worthy to be called your son; make me like one of your hired servants.'" Luke 15:17-19 NIV*

**Unclean:** *Be merciful to me, O God, because of your constant love. Because of your great mercy wipe away my sins! Wash away all my evil and make me clean from my sin! Psalm 51:1-2*

**Guilt and Sorrow:** *Peter was still down in the courtyard when one of the High Priest's servant women came by. When she saw Peter warming himself, she looked straight at him and said, "You, too, were with Jesus of Nazareth." But he denied it. "I don't know... I don't understand what you are talking about," he answered, and went out into the passageway. Just then a rooster crowed. The servant woman saw him there and began to repeat to the bystanders, "He is one of them!" But Peter denied it again. A little while later the bystanders accused Peter again, "You can't deny that you are one of them, because you, too, are* *from Galilee." Then Peter said, "I swear that I am telling the truth! May God punish me if I am not! I do not know the man you are talking about!" Just then a rooster crowed a second time, and Peter remembered how Jesus had said to him, "Before the rooster crows two times, you will say three times that you do not know me." And he broke down and cried. Mark 14: 66-72*

Our sins often result in more than just a disconnection and separation from God, they leave us with feelings of unworthiness, uncleanliness, guilt, and sorrow. In addition to separation from God, the knowledge we have of our sins often disconnects and separates us from our friends and family as well, in the form of fear of exposing our sins and feelings.

**How have you felt disconnected to other people as a result of your sins?**

_____

_____

_____

_____

**What can you do to remove those barriers of disconnection from your friends and family?**

_____

_____

_____

_____

The good news is, this disconnect was never a part of God's ultimate plan for us. God's plan involved sending his son Jesus down to earth to live a life without sin. Jesus's death on the cross built a bridge for us, mending together the disconnect we create between ourselves and God in our sinful nature.

*For sin pays its wage—death; but God's free gift is eternal life in*
*union with Christ Jesus our Lord. Romans 6:23*

Many versions of this verse are used often in church environments. I like this version specifically because it uses the word *union*. A union symbolizes the bringing together of two previously separate items. We no longer have to feel alone due to separation, because the death of Jesus gave us the gift of the Holy Spirit—God in us.

*"If you love me, keep my commands. And I will ask the Father,*
*and he will give you another advocate to help you and be with*
*you forever—the Spirit of truth. The world cannot accept him,*
*because it neither sees him nor knows him. But you know him,*
*for he lives with you and will be in you. I will not leave you as*
*orphans; I will come to you. Before long, the world will not see*
*me anymore, but you will see me. Because I live, you also will*
*live. On that day you will realize that I am in my Father, and you*
*are in me, and I am in you." John 14:15-20 NIV*

Nothing can ever again separate us from God when we have the Holy Spirit. When we feel alone in a certain situation, we are not allowing God or seeing how God wants to join us in that situation with us.

*No, in all these things we are more than conquerors through him*
*who loved us. For I am convinced that neither death nor life,*
*neither angels nor demons, neither the present nor the future,*
*nor any powers, neither height nor depth, nor anything else in*
*all creation, will be able to separate us from the love of God that*
*is in Christ Jesus our Lord. Romans 8:37-39 NIV*

**Identify any areas where you feel alone. How can you remove any barriers of disconnection and invite God into that situation with you?**

_____

_____

_____

_____

## Lesson 3: Uniqueness

What if I said none us of are as unique as we may think? Truth does reside in the fact that every one of us was made uniquely by God. Everyone as followers of God receives a unique set of talents. However, I'm going to spend this lesson focusing on the concept of feeling unique in our struggles. From something as simple as not confronting a friend about their recently changed attitude toward us, to something as deep as an addiction no one knows about, we like to keep our struggles hidden. We feel like we're the only one who understands. We feel unique—alone.

**Have you ever been in a situation where you felt as if you were going through it alone? How did you respond to that situation?**

_____

_____

_____

_____

_____

For myself, I find a direct correlation between the issues I both feel alone in and neglect to bring up in prayer. I make the same assumptions with God as I do with others. My problems are too "unique" for him.

Growing up, I was the only person in my close circle of influence who had epilepsy. I believed for years that no one was truly there *with* me because no one fully understood something that played such a large influence in my life. From the chalky taste of the chewable medicine I took that will forever be ingrained within my taste buds, to the fear of further head complications, I fought regularly with wanting to be "normal." It was obvious there was nothing I could do personally to change my reality, and with my limited knowledge of God, nothing suggested he could do anything either, so why even ask?

**What are you currently being hesitant about bringing up in prayer and why?**

_____

_____

_____

_____

_____

Over the course of more than a decade, the fear of being alone resided over me. As long as I continued to believe no one understood me or even wanted to understand me, the fear remained. In my mind, the fear I had of being alone, feeding into my shivers and nightmares, was directly related to my epilepsy. Because of my unwillingness to share my nightly struggles with others, the opportunity for seeing the way out was slim. On one hand, I was afraid of exposing the darkness I lived in. On the other, I prevented the light of Jesus from shining into my situation to bring healing. Now, I look back and see them not as a result of my condition, but as attacks and spiritual warfare from the enemy himself. The fear of being alone *never* comes from God.

> *The LORD is a refuge for the oppressed, a stronghold in times of trouble. Those who know your name trust in you, for you, LORD, have never forsaken those who seek you. Psalm 9:9-10 NIV*

God never leaves us or forsakes us. He is always there for us to cling to, even on the darkest of days. All we need to do is seek him out.

**For what reasons have you ever hesitated to bring something up in prayer?**

_____

_____

_____

_____

When we hesitate to bring issues up in prayer, we underutilize the power of prayer. This is either because we don't know the true power prayer possesses or because we just dismiss it. Realizing that our situation isn't unique to God allows us to pray with the authority that he has an answer for any subject we bring to him. What power does prayer hold?

> **Guaranteed answers:** *"For this reason I tell you: When you pray and ask for something, believe that you have received it, and you will be given whatever you ask for." Mark 11:24*
>
> **Supernatural healing:** *When Jesus saw that a crowd was running to the scene, he rebuked the impure spirit. "You deaf and mute spirit," he said, "I command you, come out of him and never enter him again." The spirit shrieked, convulsed him violently and came out. The boy looked so much like a corpse that many said, "He's dead." But Jesus took him by the hand and lifted him to his feet, and he stood up. After Jesus had gone indoors, his disciples asked him privately, "Why couldn't we drive it out?" He replied, "This kind can come out only by prayer." Mark 9:25-29 NIV*
>
> **Forgiveness of sins:** *Is anyone among you suffering? Let him pray. Is anyone cheerful? Let him sing praise. Is anyone among you sick? Let him call for the elders of the church, and let them pray over him, anointing him with oil in the name of the Lord. And the prayer of faith will save the one who is sick, and the Lord will raise him up. And if he has committed sins, he will be forgiven. James 5:13-15 ESV*

**How have you been a witness to any of these powers?**

_____

_____

_____

_____

_____

No prayer is too specific for God. The more specific our prayers, the more we will be in awe of God's power when we receive answers to those prayers. We worship a generous God who loves to provide our every need.

How would our lives change if we believed with full assurance that God answers our every need and forgives every one of our sins? God desires each of us to have the freedom produced as a result of living in that way.

> *Rejoice always, pray continually, give thanks in all circumstances; for this is God's will for you in Christ Jesus. 1 Thessalonians 5:16-18 NIV*

**What have you currently been praying for? Are you praying for it with the expectation that God will display his power to you?**

_____

_____

_____

_____

_____

**How can you expand on those prayer requests and make them more specific?**

_____

_____

_____

_____

_____

## Lesson 4: Apart

For this last lesson of the chapter, we will dig further into the word "separate" as seen in the definition of "alone" stating "separated from others."[17] The word "separate" means, "to keep apart by something intervening."[18] Depending upon its intended use, the word "apart" has opposing interpretations. The first comes with a negative connotation. We often refer to things as breaking apart, both literally and metaphorically, such as ourselves from other people and relationships. I found myself doing this frequently during childhood, not because I was better, but because I thought I was different. Effectively communicating my feelings to others was extremely difficult all throughout grade school. Alternatively, I chose to stay silent rather than spend the energy necessary for getting my point across. Why would any of my classmates want to get to know the real me enough to where they spent the same amount of energy listening to me? In my mind, they didn't. Instead, I stuck with the few good relationships I had for almost all of childhood. Regardless of whether people wanted to get to know me or not, my human nature still needed someone who was there for me.

I found that "someone" after attending youth group one Wednesday night in middle school. My struggle with loneliness or with my shivers wasn't known among the group, but God knew. I was too shy and embarrassed to let anyone know that an adolescent needed supervision to fall asleep at night due to a fear of being alone. God knew that too. Regardless of the fact that no one knew about my struggle, God cared that I knew he was there for me, and he used someone else as a resource to speak his love into my life. To do this, he had someone tell me in conversation, "We are never alone, God is always with us."

I wasn't sure whether to believe them or not, so I decided to test it out for myself—I couldn't take another night of feeling helpless. I went straight home to the place of all my fear, laid in my pitch black room, and prayed. I said, "God, if you are there, and if I am not alone, please take away my nightmares and shivers. I don't want to be alone anymore."

Sure enough, that same night, I went to bed and woke up the next day nightmare and shiver free. I had no idea what God was all about or what had

---

17  *Merriam-Webster's Dictionary and Thesaurus,* Updated Edition, s.v. "Alone."
18  *Merriam-Webster's Dictionary and Thesaurus,* Updated Edition, s.v. "Separate."

just happened to me, but I knew he was there. As a middle schooler, simply knowing God was there for me was as intimate as a relationship I needed at the time. With that in mind, I kept God as a resource that I could reach out to in further moments of desperation.

At times, setting ourselves apart can be a healthy decision. However, setting ourselves apart can also generate feelings of loneliness. The word "apart" when used in a negative context carries a bias which lends to the effect of suffering from many angles. We certainly aren't alone in these feelings. The same behaviors came up for people in the Bible as well.

*I hoped for happiness and light, but trouble and darkness came instead. I am torn apart by worry and pain; I have had day after day of suffering. Job 30:26-27*

**Think back to when you found yourself feeling like or related to the verses in Job. Did it cause you to feel alone in any way?**

_____

_____

_____

_____

As this verse indicates, we tear ourselves apart through worry and pain. This results in suffering and eventually leads to feelings of loneliness. The truth behind the verses in Job is this: anything causing the worry and pain tearing us apart is not from God. God and worry do not coexist—God is peace.

*Don't worry about anything, but in all your prayers ask God for what you need, always asking him with a thankful heart. And God's peace, which is far beyond human understanding, will keep your hearts and minds safe in union with Christ Jesus. Philippians 4:6-7*

Since God does not set us apart through worrying, we must shift how we view what it means to be set apart. The way God wants to set us apart means something radically different than how we set ourselves apart. What is the truth behind how God has set us apart?

**Apart:** *adverb* separately in place or time[19]

The Bible speaks to topic, that God has separated each of us apart at just the right places and times for a specific purpose, on multiple different occasions. Two examples in the Bible of how God set people apart are:

> *"Before I formed you in the womb I knew you, before you were born I set you apart; I appointed you as a prophet to the nations."* Jeremiah 1:5 NIV

> *"You are to be holy to me because I, the LORD, am holy, and I have set you apart from the nations to be my own."* Leviticus 20:26 NIV

Just as God told Jeremiah and Moses in those verses, each of us also has access to those promises and are set apart:

> *Therefore, if anyone cleanses himself from what is dishonorable, he will be a vessel for honorable use, set apart as holy, useful to the master of the house, ready for every good work.* 2 Timothy 2:21 ESV

**Is it hard for you to believe that God sets you apart and appoints you to do good work? If so, why?**

_____

_____

_____

_____

The verse in 2 Timothy indicates how we are a vessel for honorable use. What purpose does a vessel serve? How does being a vessel accomplish good works? Let's think for a minute about the purpose of our blood vessels. Blood vessels provide avenues for blood to flow throughout our body. By themselves, blood vessels are lifeless. When connected to the appropriate source—our heart—they become the primary avenue by which our lifeblood is distributed to our body. Just as our body's vessels distribute the blood that brings life to our physical bodies, God uses us as the vessels by which his life is distributed to his body. We are the body of Christ, and to become the person God set us apart for, we

---

19  *Merriam-Webster's Dictionary and Thesaurus,* Updated Edition, s.v. "Apart."

must connect to the source of life. Any time we disconnect from the source of everlasting life, we become just as a blood vessel would if it disconnected from our heart—lifeless. There is no back-up source for everlasting life.

> *"I am the LORD, and there is no other; apart from me there is no God. I will strengthen you, though you have not acknowledged me, so that from the rising of the sun to the place of its setting people may know there is none besides me. I am the LORD, and there is no other." Isaiah 45:5-6 NIV*

When we look at the word "apart" in the context of being set aside on this earth by God for a purpose, any feelings associated with loneliness will have no power over us. Loneliness is impossible when truly connected with someone else. Each vessel in our body is connected for a specific purpose, and each of us in the body of Christ are connected for a specific purpose as well.

**For what purpose, specifically, has God set you apart? What stops you from completing that purpose?**

_____

_____

_____

_____

**How and where can you invite God to give you the strength needed to complete your purpose?**

_____

_____

_____

_____

Dear God,

I take this time to confess any sins separating me from your good, pleasing, and perfect will for my life. I pray against any lies fed to me in an attempt to create isolation or separation among myself and other believers. You created me with the intention of being in community and companionship with others. Anything in my life breaking me apart from the church is not from you. I pray against everything causing me to condemn myself through feelings of unworthiness and guilt as a result of my sins. I ask that you fill me up with your never-ending grace and peace that comes with the knowledge of having life in union with Jesus. Thank you for being a God who walks with me through all of my struggles. There is nothing I experience on this earth that you don't know about, and my problems are never too unique for you to solve. Thank you for being a God who cares for me so much that you set me apart for a specific purpose. I ask for you to supply me with the strength needed to carry out my purpose. Reveal the direction of the path I need to be walking on in order to fulfill my purpose. I pray for your grace, power, and peace to always be enough in my life. Renew my mind to see what you set me apart for, and be the connection allowing me to combat anything preventing me from believing the truth that I am not alone.

In Jesus' name,
Amen.

## CHAPTER FOUR

# I Don't Deserve Happiness

## Introduction

The title of this chapter may have caused you to have the thought, "that is not true." If so, I want to encourage you to continue to stick with me over the course of this next set of lessons. Often times, I see people experience bitterness or have a hardened heart toward God when they go through rough seasons of life. When life throws a curve ball at us, thoughts of doubting God's goodness, like "If God loved me, this wouldn't happen," or "If God was real, why did he put me through this situation?" begin to surface in our minds. In those times of doubt, involvement in a community is critical. A community of others who are also seeking out God's truth, not a community of others who only tell us to "think happier thoughts."

Thoughts of doubting God's goodness rarely, if ever, occur when we are experiencing happiness and life is going "our way." The concept of wanting happiness itself is not bad, quite the contrary, wanting happiness can be *great*. However, there are many things we gain from going through difficult seasons in life. If we go through those seasons always looking for the happiness on the other side, we miss out greatly on the lessons God wants to teach us in those situations. An improper desire for happiness can create the potential to spend significant amounts of time looking for happiness from the wrong things and in the wrong places. This chapter addresses that issue and will focus on things, such as: why we strive for happiness, what it means to desire happiness, and how God fulfills our craving for happiness.

## Lesson 1: Deserving

From the moment I prayed to receive God in my life during middle school and for the next few years, God remained as the person I went to only in situations when I felt I deserved better. For example, I had no control over the fact that I had nightmares regularly as a child. I wasn't doing anything to encourage them, and I certainly didn't invite them back in on my own accord. When I finally made the prayer asking God to take them away, he did. I also had no control over the fact that I have epilepsy. I can't count how many times I sat in frustration over it, and to this day, I still take medicine for it. As it stands, God took one of my trials away and not the other, why is that? I don't deserve to live with things that are outside of my control, right?

Our society constantly asks the question, "Why do bad things happen to good people?" When unfortunate circumstances happen, we say "I'm sorry, you didn't *deserve* to go through that." But, how much truth exists in that last statement? When we treat God as a person we call on only in times of desperation and perceived unfairness, we completely miss the essence of God. If we only ask God for guidance and supplication in moments of feeling we deserve better, we treat him as if he is our servant rather than a Father. God desires to take care of us at all times and always uses the circumstances outside of our control for his glory, why not ask him how he plans to use our circumstances instead of focusing on how he can change them?

At the end of the day, whether we think we deserve something or not, or whether those bad things happen to good or bad people, we are *all* still sinful people. What does it mean to deserve?

**Deserve:** *verb* to be worthy of: merit[20]

What does our sin make us worthy of?

*For the wages of sin is death, but the gift of God is eternal life in Christ Jesus our Lord. Romans 6:23 NIV*

The penalty we deserve to pay for our sins is death. The initial thought of that consequence likely feels very defeating. Death and feeling defeated was never God's ultimate plan for us, God already knew what our actions

20  *Merriam-Webster's Dictionary and Thesaurus,* Updated Edition, s.v. "Deserve."

would merit. As a result, he constructed a plan to bring forth a revolution of eternal life.

That verse also states that God gifted us eternal life through his son Jesus. Let that sink in for a moment—God loves each of us so much, he provided us with a way to eternal life through the death of his son Jesus so that we may forever be with him. Why does Paul state it as being a gift?

What intentions arise when we think of presenting someone with a gift? A few characteristics associated with the process of what it takes to truly give a gift to a person are:

✦ Having someone other than ourselves on our mind
✦ Paying the price the gift and not expecting the other person to pay us back
✦ Giving the gift for a specific reason or at a particular event in time

**What does it mean to you that God gifted you with eternal life?**

_____

_____

_____

_____

_____

**How does looking at a gift from those perspectives change the way you look at God gifting you with eternal life?**

_____

_____

_____

_____

_____

God keeps us on his mind *all of the time*, Jesus paid the price for *all of our sins*, and *no pay back* on our end is expected. Through the death of Jesus, we can receive the gifts of eternal life and the Holy Spirit.

**Have you received the gift of the Holy Spirit? If so, how has your life changed as a result?**

_____

_____

_____

_____

## Lesson 2: Striving

Everywhere we turn, messages of achieving happiness surround us. They are so common, that sometimes we can feel like there is something wrong with us if we aren't happy. In their effort to "make things right," those messages aim to convince us how they possess the formula for what it takes to obtain that happiness. In some messages, the answer lies just one click away from buying their special product. In others, it lives in a class or a seminar that shows the way to new happiness. If we're already happy with the way our life is currently, we more than likely ignore these messages. If we're not, we are more apt to search outside of ourselves to find an answer. Often times, our search for happiness takes place without us even knowing what we're truly searching for. All we know is we want happiness, and we want it *now*.

Talk about an amazing place for Satan to leverage his ability to manipulate! If we just stick to a habit long enough, we'll all get to where we want to be, right? Not necessarily. We will all arrive at places in life where our current state no longer seems like enough.

After grade school, I arrived at a similar place with God. He was great as a person who performed miracles when I asked him to, but I needed something more meaningful now—a deeper level of intimacy in a relationship. I was no longer happy with the surface-level-helper God was for me. I had no clue

God desired to have the same closeness with me, and because of my lack of knowledge, I began looking for it elsewhere. All of a sudden, I found myself doing anything I felt appropriate in order to feel happy. I reached desperation. I encountered a relational void, and gravitated toward drinking alcohol in order to not feel that void, just so I could be "happy" for a moment again. What do we strive for in those moments?

**Happy:** *adjective* enjoying well-being and contentment[21]

Focusing on the "contentment" portion of happiness, what spurs the feeling of contentment? Is striving for contentment life-giving? I find two main reasons for which we become content. The first? We don't want to grow, we're pretty happy with where we see life taking us, and we have no reason to change. The other? We don't care enough, and the less invested we are in an issue, the more content we are no matter what result comes out of the issue.

**What areas in your life do you feel content in right now?**

_____

_____

_____

_____

**What areas in your life do you feel God may be asking you to work on right now?**

_____

_____

_____

_____

---

21  *Merriam-Webster's Dictionary and Thesaurus,* Updated Edition, s.v. "Happy."

Were there any of the same or closely related areas listed in both of those questions? God cares about every single one of us too much for him to stay content. The outcome of our eternal life contains so much value to him that he invested the death of his son as assurance of giving us a choice to spend our eternity with him. I'm going to guess that personal happiness wasn't a concern for Jesus leading up to the suffering he endured during his death on the cross. At the same time, Jesus cared too much about each one of us to approach the situation differently.

What did Jesus strive for? Jesus came to this earth with one mission: to do everything God, his Father, told him to do.

> *Jesus gave them this answer: "Very truly I tell you, the Son can do nothing by himself; he can do only what he sees his Father doing, because whatever the Father does the Son also does. For the Father loves the Son and shows him all he does. Yes, and he will show him even greater works than these, so that you will be amazed." John 5:19-20 NIV*

Contentment becomes what we experience when we try to contain the amount in which we allow God to work within us. Considering this, it is no surprise that just at the time we begin to feel content in something, God says "ok, time for the next step." Frequently, we overlook experiencing growth opportunities in our relationship with God because either we won't step out of our comfort zone, or because we're too focused on striving for a different reality during times of suffering. How does the Bible speak into this topic?

> *The righteous person may have many troubles, but the LORD delivers him from them all; Psalm 34:19 NIV*

**How would it look different if you approached the troubles you faced by looking at how God wants to deliver you from them rather than focusing on how much better things could be?**

---

---

---

---

*For our light and momentary troubles are achieving for us
an eternal glory that far outweighs them all. 2 Corinthians
4:17 NIV*
*Don't be afraid of your enemies; always be courageous, and
this will prove to them that they will lose and that you will win,
because it is God who gives you the victory. For you have been
given the privilege of serving Christ, not only by believing in
him, but also by suffering for him. Philippians 1:28-29*

**Have you ever looked at a time of suffering as a privilege you've been
given for the purpose of serving Christ?**

_____

_____

_____

_____

I specifically like the wording in the verse from Philippians, and see it
ring true in almost every single testimony any friend shares with me. Think
about it personally, how many stories of people coming to Christ resulted
from the biggest trials they both experienced and overcame? My guess is a
lot of them.

**If God works through suffering and uses times of suffering to serve for
his glory, why would you want to overlook those times in search for
happiness?**

_____

_____

_____

_____

**How have you seen God deliver you from times of suffering faced in your own life?**

_____

_____

_____

_____

_____

## Lesson 3: Desires

How would the world look differently if the desires of our hearts matched God's desires for us? In my experience, most human desires are to be more *alike* something else, and God's desire is for us to be more *unique*. When we see attributes another person possesses that we don't, we become prone to falling into a state of jealousy. We desire to be more like them. At the same time, God watches over us and holds the strongest desire for each of us to be the unique person he created us as.

I find in most cases, these desires of ours become heightened during times of distress. Moving hours away from all of my life-long friends to go to college created extreme relational distress within me. I was determined not to fall back into the states of loneliness and fear I had as a child. I put the pressure all on myself to find the right new friends and I went to any party I was invited to in order to meet them. When we feel the pain and pressure from a hard time weighing down on us, we suddenly become much more passionate about the outcome of those situations.

We don't like going through sustained periods of rough times. For the flesh, it almost becomes our second nature to desire happiness during those times. But is happiness what we really want? I would argue that what we truly search for is not happiness, but rather joy.

**Is it possible for that relationship to exist the other way around? Can being happy bring upon joy?**

_____

_____

_____

_____

_____

The majority of the time, we use the words "joy" or "happiness," almost interchangeably. Are they interchangeable in meaning?

**Joy:** *noun* a source of happiness[22]

At the core of happiness and joy lie drastically different meanings. I specifically like how it states that joy is the *source*. This indicates that happiness results from joy, not the other way around. In the world of chemistry, indicators such as acid-base indicators are added to solutions in order to indicate the concentration of hydrogen ions a solution. There isn't just one acid-base indicator to rule all indicators. Multiple compounds possess the qualities of an acid-base indicator. The indicator chosen for an experiment depends on the nature of the solution.

Similarly, happiness isn't the only indicator to reveal the presence of joy. Depending on the nature of our circumstances, the presence of joy serves as the source for multiple states. Joy is multi-faceted, and the relationship between happiness and joy is *not* interchangeable. Joy is the source and happiness is the one of the effects we experience as a result of joy. Looking at the Bible, we see how it speaks about joy from many different aspects.

Joy is:

**Glorious:** *You love him, although you have not seen him, and you believe in him, although you do not now see him. So you rejoice with a great and glorious joy which words cannot express, because you are receiving the salvation of your souls, which is the purpose of your faith in him. 1 Peter 1:8-9*

---

22    *Merriam-Webster's Dictionary and Thesaurus,* Updated Edition, s.v. "Joy."

**Strong**: *Nehemiah said, "Go and enjoy choice food and sweet drinks, and send some to those who have nothing prepared. This day is holy to our Lord. Do not grieve, for the joy of the LORD is your strength." Nehemiah 8:10 NIV*
**Enduring**: *...fixing our eyes on Jesus, the pioneer and perfecter of faith. For the joy set before him he endured the cross, scorning its shame, and sat down at the right hand of the throne of God. Hebrews 12:2 NIV*
**Permanent**: *"So with you: Now is your time of grief, but I will see you again and you will rejoice, and no one will take away your joy." John 16:22 NIV*

Joy brings immeasurably more to us than happiness ever will. Yet, we continue to run our lives by the measure of happiness or pleasure that we obtain. Once that happiness fades, we revisit the problem and perpetuate habits to bring momentary restoration. Before we know it, an idol in our life comes to existence. Some of these habits are inherently "good" things. I really enjoy being around people and serving them, but if I begin to find my happiness only in those people and allow them to draw my attention and focus away from God, I create an idol.

However, more often than not, our habits get formed from things that aren't so "good." Once I initiated a search for new friends and stronger relationships, my pursuit of a life of partying was just beginning. I wanted relationships that offered the strong, enduring, glorious, and permanent solution joy offers. Instead, I received a temporary happiness every time I drank and met people in my inebriated state. For most of those people, their only interest in hanging out was if we were going to drink again. This is likely because deep down, they searched for the same things in the same ways I did and they needed their happiness restored too.

**What in your life brings you joy?**

_____

_____

_____

**If you aren't already doing so, how might you use those things to draw you closer to God?**

_____

_____

_____

At the end of the day, true joy comes from God. He provides us with everlasting joy through the Holy Spirit.

> *But the Spirit produces love, joy, peace, patience, kindness,*
> *goodness, faithfulness, humility, and self-control. There is no*
> *law against such things as these. Galatians 5:22-23*

Just as happiness is one of the many indicators of joy, joy is one of the many indicators of being filled with the Holy Spirit. God loves to use joy not just in the happy times, but in times of suffering as well. On one hand, the results of pursuing joy in times of suffering are both closeness to him and strength in our relationship with him. On the other hand, the devil uses our times of suffering to convince us to distance ourselves away from God. The enemy whispers to us, surely our answer can be found elsewhere, right?

> *Consider it pure joy, my brothers and sisters, whenever you face*
> *trials of many kinds, because you know that the testing of your*
> *faith produces perseverance. James 1:2-3 NIV*

Note that the verse in James above doesn't say *if* we face trials of many kinds, it says when. Trials in this life are inevitable. Satan knows each of us will encounter trials. Those trials present the perfect place for Satan to attack us with the lie that happiness is a better answer.

**What steps can you take toward experiencing joy in times of suffering?**

_____

_____

_____

**Have you found joy in any past sufferings? If so, what emotions resulted from it and how did it strengthen your relationship with God?**

_____

_____

_____

_____

<p align="center">~~~∞∞∞~~~</p>

## Lesson 4: Satisfaction and Fulfillment

When it comes to fulfillment and what it means to fulfill, the first thought to pop in my mind is on fulfilling a set of standards. The moment each variable in a set of standards is met, we have officially fulfilled whatever we are pursuing. When a set of standards remains unfulfilled, it can cause us to experience a void. We become dissatisfied. This theme is common when searching the realm of happiness. Often times, when we do things to bring us happiness, what we're actually searching for is something to satisfy or fulfill us. The product of our satisfaction and fulfillment becomes happiness, and once the satisfaction or fulfillment wears off, we go back looking for more. If this pattern continues, we begin to form a dependence. If our dependence is on anything other than God, the "fulfillment" we receive from it _will_ be temporary.

Every time I drank, I received a fulfillment of social interaction from the people at the same parties, but it was only as temporary as how long I could hold my own before blacking out. It didn't take much for people to start talking when I was in a room loud enough to drown out the reality behind me, and the people were too drunk to care about my personality quirks. If I was willing to drink, they were willing to talk.

> _So we fix our eyes not on what is seen, but on what is unseen, since what is seen is temporary, but what is unseen is eternal. 2 Corinthians 4:18 NIV_

What is fulfillment?

**Fulfill:** _verb_ to meet the requirements of: satisfy[23]

---

23  _Merriam-Webster's Dictionary and Thesaurus,_ Updated Edition, s.v. "Fulfill."

What requirements need satisfying? In the Old Testament, those requirements were outlined in what is commonly referred to as the Law. The only problem with the requirements in the Law is that none of us will ever come close to fulfilling them. God, being the gracious Father he is, knew we couldn't fulfill them well in advance and crafted a plan for us to achieve community with him. The Old Testament is flooded with verses speaking to the coming of a savior: Jesus. Jesus carried out God's Law and brought to realization what none of us will ever accomplish.

> *"Do not think that I have come to abolish the Law or the Prophets; I have not come to abolish them but to fulfill them." Matthew 5:17 NIV*

What requirements do we need to satisfy now that Jesus came to fulfill the Law? There is only one—to believe in Jesus. Jesus = fulfillment.

> *Then they asked him, "What must we do to do the works God requires?" Jesus answered, "The work of God is this: to believe in the one he has sent." John 6:28-29 NIV*

Jesus is the only one who lived a life in fulfillment to the Law. Any time we fail to put our faith in Jesus and his fulfillment of the Law, we fall into a "works-based" faith. Every second where Jesus stops being enough and we find ourselves longing for answers elsewhere, we water down what Jesus did for us on the cross. Sure, we can fill our lives with substances, but none of those substances will fill us like the water Jesus provides for us.

> *Jesus answered, "Everyone who drinks this water will be thirsty again, but whoever drinks the water I give them will never thirst. Indeed, the water I give them will become in them a spring of water welling up to eternal life." John 4:13-14 NIV*

**What do you find yourself doing when seeking fulfillment?**

_____

_____

_____

_____

*As for you, you were dead in your transgressions and sins, in which you used to live when you followed the ways of this world and of the ruler of the kingdom of the air, the spirit who is now at work in those who are disobedient. All of us also lived among them at one time, gratifying the cravings of our flesh and following its desires and thoughts. Like the rest, we were by nature deserving of wrath. But because of his great love for us, God, who is rich in mercy, made us alive with Christ even when we were dead in transgressions—it is by grace you have been saved. Ephesians 2:1-5 NIV*

**How do you feel knowing you can't do anything to earn the fulfillment Jesus brings?**

_____

_____

_____

_____

For some of us, the thought that nothing we can do to earn fulfillment makes us uncomfortable at first, but why? Likely, because everything we receive in an earthly sense is given to us by first doing something to "earn" or "deserve" it.

I spent years after high school trying to earn people's favor. However, I couldn't earn that favor unless I first gave them reason to feel I deserved their attention. Always out to prove myself, I gave them that "something." I side with David in regards to stature, but I could compete drink-for-drink with the Goliath of any party, and I did. To say I got people's attention is an understatement. I not only got their attention, I got their favor too. The only condition? To sustain that favor, I had to repeat my Goliath efforts every time I walked into a party. The second I underperformed, their expectations remained unmet, and they became dissatisfied.

What's the difference between earthly fulfillment and the fulfillment of Jesus? There is no work we can ever accomplish to receive fulfillment from God. The last part of those verses states *only* by God's grace are we saved, *not by works!* In Jesus lies freedom. We no longer have to perform, but simply believe in Jesus.

It is imperative that we as a community of believers continually encourage one another. The influences of the world surrounding us daily cause us to slip into the mindset of feeling like we need to earn God's fulfillment.

**What steps can you take right now to lead *yourself* in the direction of the fulfillment only found in God?**

_____

_____

_____

_____

**What steps can you take right now to lead *others* in the direction of the fulfillment only found in God?**

_____

_____

_____

_____

Dear God,

I confess I am a sinful human being and acknowledge the wages of my sin is death. Thank you for being a God who loves me so much, that you paid the price of my sin to reunite me with you through your Holy Spirit. Thank you for being a God who not only wants unity with me, but also desires a relationship with me. Show me areas of my life where my contentment keeps me from expanding my faith in you. Supply me with a mindset that all things I go through are for your glory, and that my sufferings are a privilege given to me for the purpose of following you. If I ever look for happiness, guide me first in the direction of joy—a glorious, strong, enduring, permanent, joy found only through your Holy Spirit. Expose any idols I create in my life that draw me away from your fulfillment, and show me how to encourage those around me to actively seek the fulfillment only you provide.

In Jesus' name,
Amen.

## CHAPTER FIVE

# I Am Useful

## Lesson 1: Of Good Effect

What good is this doing for me? We've all asked ourselves that question before. Whether we sit in a meeting that we feel is a waste of our time, are being lectured to about a subject we already know, or we simply fail to see the point of what we're being told to do, we want to see the benefit from what we do.

When we don't see the good outcome of an event, we start to ask questions like, "If nothing good comes out of this, why would I do it?" and "What value does this bring me?" When good is brought out of our environment and circumstances, it allows us to also see the usefulness of them.

Similar to how we desire to see the usefulness of areas that we invest our time and energy in, we also desire to see and feel our usefulness as a person. When we see an object's usefulness, we subconsciously assign it with a certain amount of importance. We associate higher values to objects we find of use. Where does that value come from? How is the amount in which we are of use measured?

> **Useful:** *adjective* being of use or service; serving some purpose; advantageous, helpful, or of good effect; of practical use, as for doing work; producing material results; supplying common needs[24]

Looking further into the "of good effect" portion, it is imperative that we recognize usefulness of the good *effect* it brings, not the *cause*. This

---

24  *Dictionary.com,* s.v. "Useful," accessed November 1, 2018, https://www.dictionary.com/

suggests that in general, the limit of our willingness to invest in an outcome is endless when we know the good effect it brings. One of the most important investments we can make is the investment in ourselves. We must be conscious of our own good effect—our usefulness. If we start to doubt our usefulness, we can become unable to see the good effect we bring and in return devalue ourselves.

**Where in your life are you currently unable to see the good you bring?**

_____

_____

_____

_____

Our personal stories are unique from any human-authored book we've read because we don't know what the end looks like. We can't flip ahead in the pages to find out spoilers along the way. In other words, we often don't know the fullness of the long-term _good effect_ our life's story provides. Which brings us to the question: Are we able to know that our story will have a good effect at all? The answer is, "yes." God makes it a promise to each of his followers to use our stories for good.

> _And we know that in all things God works for the good of those who love him, who have been called according to his purpose._
> _Romans 8:28 NIV_

**What prevents you from truly believing God works all things for good?**

_____

_____

_____

_____

**Can you think of a past situation in your life where God worked everything out for good?**

_____

_____

_____

_____

In order to know the truth that our story will have a good effect, we have to trust God to author our story. The verse above in Romans tells us that God uses *all things* for good, no matter how bad we perceive what we did.

For the better part of two years, I spent almost as many nights drunk as I did sober. As soon as Thursday evening hit, the weekly 3-day partying stint began. After the decisions of whose house where pre-gaming would take place, which club we'd go to after, and who would be my buddy for the evening, it was game on. Once the alcohol masked my desperation for a genuine relationship just enough, the party began. I gauged my usefulness off of how long I kept up drink for drink with my friends, and making it to as many parties as possible. As a person who highly values actions, I stopped at nothing to make sure I "showed up" for my friends and proved to others at the party that "I could hang."

If I had justified back then why I partook in those events, my answer would have been that it brought me some level of value. The "good effect" from it became all of the friends I would party with in the future. The terrible effect was letting myself get to the point where I created a dependence on alcohol—a dependence that resulted in me waking up hungover the next day, ashamed from getting so drunk that I'd vomit and need to be escorted to my bed, yet another night.

The only person who wants us to feel shame is Satan. Before Eve committed the first sin in the garden, Adam and Eve resided in the garden with God and shame did not exist.

> *Adam and his wife were both naked, and they felt no shame.*
> *Genesis 2:25 NIV*

Shame is *not from God.* For as long as we allow God to author our story, we never have reason to fear that our investments aren't being used for good. God invested his son's life to ensure that our story would have a good effect. The transaction is finished.

Just as any human author has a well thought-out plan for any story they write, God has a well thought-out plan for our lives. As any good story entails, he will not reveal something in our story until it reaches the point in the story where it makes the most sense. This principle is seen in the following verses:

> *For we are God's handiwork, created in Christ Jesus to do good works, which God prepared in advance for us to do. Ephesians 2:10 NIV*
>
> *Whoever sows to please their flesh, from the flesh will reap destruction; whoever sows to please the Spirit, from the Spirit will reap eternal life. Let us not become weary in doing good, for at the proper time we will reap a harvest if we do not give up. Galatians 6:8-9 NIV*

The hardest part about allowing God to author our story is the element of faith. Maintaining faith and trusting in God are crucial if we want to experience the fullness of the good effect God has for our story. The moment we begin to lose faith, we begin making edits to the story God is writing. We live in one chapter and begin to doubt that God will introduce the character we're looking for, so we try to write them in ourselves instead. Although God does use all of our own edits in our stories for good, those edits often come as an effect of us veering off of the path of the story God has for us and finding our way back to that path.

God is good, all the time, and so is every story written by him. We are all useful in our own unique way. The only thing left for us to do is to have faith and submit our lives accordingly to the one and only perfect author.

**What causes you to doubt God's timing on events in your story?**

_____

_____

_____

_____

**Does knowing God prepared works in advance for you to do help give you peace around events in your story? Why or why not?**

_____

_____

_____

_____

~~~~~~~~

## Lesson 2: Practical Work

During the summer following my freshman year of college, I took an internship selling cable and internet packages door-to-door. When working in sales, a critical element to master is communicating to consumers how they can find use in your product. However, a unique problem of selling cable and internet packages versus many other products people sell door-to-door, is the lack of having a physical product to show. Without a physical product, communicating the product's usefulness becomes much more difficult.

Upon navigating the tricks of the trade quickly, I climbed my way to the top-ten earning representatives in the Midwest region and earned myself the office nickname "E-money." I achieved rapid success by perfecting the impulse factor of indifference. It didn't matter to me how or where my sales came from, I knew if I stayed true to myself and talked to enough people, I would make sales. I leveraged the art of practical communication to display the use of my product. Those skills came as a result of mastering my pitch and asking the right questions. Questions such as, "What are your favorite TV channels?" and "How many TV's do you have?" When I had received that information, presenting how my services could better fit their family's needs was a piece of cake.

Relating this to this angle of "useful" which is, "of practical use, as for doing work,"[25] we see how usefulness is directly correlated to our ability to see an item's practicality. When we deem any product or process as "impractical," it is likely because it doesn't give us anything we don't already have for a

---

25    *Dictionary.com,* s.v. "Useful," accessed November 1, 2018, https://www.dictionary.com/

better value. What happens when we look at this concept of practicality in the context of our personal story, is the work we do of any use?

**Do you know what your story is working toward? If so, what? If not, how can you ask God to assist you along the way?**

_____

_____

_____

> **Practical:** _adjective_ consisting of, involving, or resulting from practice or action[26]

Since we know things coined as useful are of practical use, and we know that practicality comes from putting things into practice, what should be practicing? Putting actions into practice is commonly spoken of in the Bible, in the forms of:

> **God's Commands:** _"Do not think that I have come to abolish the Law or the Prophets; I have not come to abolish them but to fulfill them. For truly I tell you, until heaven and earth disappear, not the smallest letter, not the least stroke of a pen, will by any means disappear from the Law until everything is accomplished. Therefore anyone who sets aside one of the least of these commands and teaches others accordingly will be called least in the kingdom of heaven, but whoever practices and teaches these commands will be called great in the kingdom of heaven." Matthew 5:17-19 NIV_

> **God's Word:** _"Therefore everyone who hears these words of mine and puts them into practice is like a wise man who built his house on the rock. The rain came down, the streams rose, and the winds blew and beat against that house; yet it did not fall, because it had its foundation on the rock." Matthew 7:24-25 NIV_

> **Hospitality:** _Never be lacking in zeal, but keep your spiritual fervor, serving the Lord. Be joyful in hope, patient in affliction,_

---

26  _Dictionary.com_, s.v. "Practical," accessed November 1, 2018, https://www.dictionary.com/

*faithful in prayer. Share with the Lord's people who are in need.*
*Practice hospitality. Romans 12:11-13 NIV*

Practicing God's word, his teachings, and hospitality will always contain use. God intends for us to use every word of his teachings as a resource for drawing us closer to him, or it wouldn't be included in the Bible. We exist on this earth to serve him and share his good news with all of God's people who are in need.

**Between following God's commands, spending time in the word, and practicing hospitality, which do you find hardest to do and why?**

_____

_____

_____

**Do any of these things come easily to you? How can you encourage others around you to do the same?**

_____

_____

_____

**How can you continue to practice, grow, and learn in these areas? Are you surrounding yourself with people who do these things regularly so you can continue to practice, grow, and learn from them?**

_____

_____

_____

_____

## Lesson 3: Producing Results

We come into contact with advertisements daily, trying to convince us to buy products based on their ability to produce results. The more compelling the argument, the more people find use in the product. Advertisements that are able to prove a product's ability to produce results are commonly used as an effective way to communicate usefulness. We live in a society that feeds off of quick and easily recognizable change. When people post transformational photos of themselves from a diet or exercise plan they executed, the faster they accomplished their results, the more impressed we are and likely, our willingness to also try it increases.

From a results-producing standpoint, we often gauge the usefulness based off of the quantity of results produced. However, in the definition "producing material results,"[27] we see no indication of the quantity produced. How does producing results change meaning when the word "material" is added?

> **Material:** *noun* a group of ideas, facts, data, etc., that may provide the basis for or be incorporated into some integrated work[28]

God uses humans as the material for completing his work here on earth. The combination of materials we have to use in our story is something only we possess. Depending upon a limitless number of variables, the ideas, facts, and data we collect along the way is unique to any other human story written. Our experiences and each of our stories are used as materials to equip us for bringing God's will here on earth as it is in heaven.

> *Now may the God of peace who brought again from the dead our Lord Jesus, the great shepherd of the sheep, by the blood of the eternal covenant, equip you with everything good that you may do his will, working in us that which is pleasing in his sight, through Jesus Christ, to whom be glory forever and ever. Amen. Hebrews 13:20-21 ESV*

---

27  *Dictionary.com,* s.v. "Useful," accessed November 1, 2018, https://www.dictionary.com/
28  *Dictionary.com,* s.v. "Material," accessed November 1, 2018, https://www.dictionary.com/

**How do you view your story as a material that God both uses and incorporates into his will being done?**

_____

_____

_____

_____

**What good things has God equipped you with to do his will?**

_____

_____

_____

_____

**How do you use those good things to do God's will for your story?**

_____

_____

_____

_____

Now that we know God's intention is to use us all as materials to be integrated into his work, let's focus on the results-producing aspect. How do the results produced from things of this world versus things from God differ? From the worldly perspective, the results are always temporal.

When I pursued a life of partying in college, I searched for fulfillment. Fulfillment in entertainment, relationships, and acceptance. I repeated the same routine of seeking entertainment by getting drunk, and craving relationships and acceptance from everyone at the parties to have people to do it with all over again the next week. In reality, I became the entertainment by throwing back enough drinks to dominate any beer pong table. After a certain amount of drinks, my mental capacity could only focus on one thing without passing out, and that was the group of cups sitting at the other end of the table. No one could distract me from getting "on fire." The most sustaining relationship I made was with the bathroom, that is if I was lucky enough to make it there before throwing up, and the only acceptance I had inside was accepting the fact that I still hadn't found the relationship I was searching for.

In the morning, the feeling of drunkenness would wear off and my external acceptance would only return if I partook in the same activities. The results I produced were different every night, and only lasted long enough to make it to the next party a couple days later.

Unlike the temporal results that the things of this world produce, results produced from a spiritual aspect are everlasting. What results get produced from using what God equips us with to do his will?

> *When you were slaves to sin, you were free from the control of righteousness. What benefit did you reap at that time from the things you are now ashamed of? Those things result in death! But now that you have been set free from sin and have become slaves of God, the benefit you reap leads to holiness, and the result is eternal life. For the wages of sin is death, but the gift of God is eternal life in Christ Jesus our Lord. Romans 6:20-23 NIV*

From those verses we see the two types of results produced: eternal life, or death. When we become a slave to sin, the result produced is death. When we become a slave to God, we find eternal life. Although the word "slave" often carries a bad connotation based on the context of its use, however it also means:

> **Slave:** *noun* a person entirely under the domination of some influence or person[29]

In this context, we are the person and the two influences are either God or sin. Which leads to the question: which influence do we allow to take effect in our life?

---

29  *Dictionary.com,* s.v. "Slave," accessed November 1, 2018, https://www.dictionary.com/

When I allowed my life to be controlled by the sin of drunkenness, the results were anything but life-sustaining. I woke up empty every morning, and yet fulfilled just enough the night before to continue pursuing my sin to the point that it enslaved me.

Pursuing God as the influence over my life has redeemed everything which once brought emptiness. It now all carries a purpose for being a material in my story God writes. What once seemed useless now carries use every time I share my testimony. God is all about redemption. He brings each of us who were once dead to our sins back to life through Jesus's death on the cross. It's as simple as admitting we don't have it all together and allowing his influence to permeate our lives.

**What areas of your life are currently under the control of sin? What results are produced in those areas of your life?**

_____

_____

_____

_____

_____

**What areas of your life are under the influence of God? What results are produced in those areas?**

_____

_____

_____

_____

_____

## Lesson 4: Supplying Needs

As humans who exist on this earth, we come with a list of basic needs for survival. Over the course of time, how those needs are met has drastically changed. One of those basic needs is the need for community. In the days of the hunter-gatherers, a community helped the odds of one's ability to eat and survive. In the world today, communities from all over the world come together around similar spiritual, social, and entertainment interests. The basic human need of community and the increased number of available resources to meet those needs comes with a list of additional perceived needs such as having a cell phone and access to social media. While cell phones themselves possess nothing we need for survival that cannot be found elsewhere, their extreme convenience and usefulness for communication easily sells us on their value. I don't think I need to sell to anyone the value cell phones have in our society today. But, are we looking for value in the right places?

Just as we use cell phones to help supply our need for communication, our stories have use in supplying the basic needs of others. In order to understand how much God uses our story in this capacity, we must first understand our true needs. The Bible lays the foundation for describing those needs, some of which are commonly known material needs, such as:

> **Food:** *When the Israelites saw it, they said to each other, "What is it?" For they did not know what it was. Moses said to them, "It is the bread the LORD has given you to eat. This is what the LORD has commanded: 'Everyone is to gather as much as they need. Take an omer for each person you have in your tent.'"* Exodus 16:15-16 NIV

> **Clothing:** *"For I was hungry and you gave me something to eat, I was thirsty and you gave me something to drink, I was a stranger and you invited me in, I needed clothes and you clothed me, I was sick and you looked after me, I was in prison and you came to visit me." Matthew 25:35-36 NIV*

Having the needs of food and clothing isn't news for any of us. But, not having those needs met could be news. The resources we now have in this world to produce food and clothing makes supplying those needs easier than ever before. It can enable us to overlook the fact that those needs aren't always met for everyone in our circle of influence. Numerous organizations exist around the world to ensure that the reach of meeting of those needs spans as wide as possible. For some of us, a huge part of our God-written story includes meeting those basic needs for others. For others, our usefulness comes in the form of meeting the non-material-based needs of the world, such as:

**Healing:** *When the teachers of the law who were Pharisees saw him eating with the sinners and tax collectors, they asked his disciples: "Why does he eat with tax collectors and sinners?" On hearing this, Jesus said to them, "It is not the healthy who need a doctor, but the sick. I have not come to call the righteous, but sinners." Mark 2:16-17 NIV*

**Mercy:** *Do not hold against us the sins of past generations; may your mercy come quickly to meet us, for we are in desperate need. Psalm 79:8 NIV*

**Jesus:** *Jesus, then, is the High Priest that meets our needs. He is holy; he has no fault or sin in him; he has been set apart from sinners and raised above the heavens. He is not like other high priests; he does not need to offer sacrifices every day for his own sins first and then for the sins of the people. He offered one sacrifice, once and for all, when he offered himself. Hebrews 7:26-27*

**How are non-material needs currently met for you and for those around you?**

_____

_____

_____

**How are non-material needs currently *not* met for you and for those around you?**

_____

_____

_____

We all have the ability to both display mercy and be the hands and feet of Jesus to those around us. God uses all of us who are willing to be used by him to act as the avenue by which these needs are met around the world.

> Then Jesus came to them and said, "All authority in heaven and on earth has been given to me. Therefore go and make disciples of all nations, baptizing them in the name of the Father and of the Son and of the Holy Spirit, and teaching them to obey everything I have commanded you. And surely I am with you always, to the very end of the age." Matthew 28:18-20 NIV

As stated above in the passage commonly known as "The Great Commission," we are all called to make disciples and teach others about him. What does it look like to supply those needs?

**Supply:** *verb* to furnish or provide (a person, establishment, place, etc.) with what is lacking or requisite[30]

During the years that I was drinking to excess, I was blind to my needs for healing, mercy, and Jesus. I knew I had needs, and I knew the need I wanted most was a relationship of greater intimacy than any I had already. Every time I tried to meet that need at a party, I came up short. I sinned on purpose by getting drunk, and I didn't care that I was sinning because my unmet needs required supplication. To get the relationship I wanted, I needed to take off the mask I put on by drinking. The problem was, I was blind to my true identity beneath the mask. I needed someone committed enough to pursue a relationship with me despite all I lacked—I needed Jesus.

Many of us have this story. We have needs that must be fulfilled. Dependent upon the severity of our needs, the more desperate we become to fulfill them. My need to be known intimately remained vacant until someone fulfilled The Great Commission with their own life and redirected me toward Jesus. Along with my redirection, I received a plethora of mercy. I knew my excessive drinking was wrong, and I knew I didn't deserve favor because of it. It took a couple of years until the right person came into my life and loved me in spite of my purposeful sinning before I would agree to better alternatives. I told myself that I wasn't an easy person to love, and it took someone showing me what the love of Jesus looks like to change my ways.

That display of love from the other person did not come without a cost to them. Any time we supply someone with a need, it requires some element of sacrifice on our end.

---

30  *Dictionary.com*, s.v. "Supply," accessed November 1, 2018, https://www.dictionary.com/

Whether it comes from our time, energy, resources, money, etc., people need to be *invested* in by us. If we pursue those investments with the uncertainty of how we will be replenished with the resources that we supply to others, it generates a community of fearful givers, rather than the community of cheerful givers the Bible calls us to be.

> *The point is this: whoever sows sparingly will also reap sparingly, and whoever sows bountifully will also reap bountifully. Each one must give as he has made up his mind, not reluctantly or under compulsion, for God loves a cheerful giver. And God is able to make all grace abound to you, so that having all sufficiency in all things at all times, you may abound in every good work. As it is written, "He has distributed freely, he has given to the poor; his righteousness endures forever." He who supplies seed to the sower and bread for food will supply and multiply your seed for sowing and increase the harvest of your righteousness. You will be enriched in every way for all your generosity, which through us will produce thanksgiving to God. For the ministry of this service is not only supplying the needs of the saints, but is also overflowing in many thanksgivings to God. 2 Corinthians 9:6-12 ESV*

This passage tells us when we supply the needs of others, not only are seeds we use to supply those needs replenished, they become multiplied, and give us more than what we started with. We have the ability to show acts of thanksgiving to God through supplying the needs of others.

**What fears do you have that prevent you from giving cheerfully?**

_____

_____

_____

_____

_____

**How has God previously used you to supply the needs of others?**

_____

_____

_____

_____

**How has God enriched you because of your generosity in supplying the needs of others?**

_____

_____

_____

_____

Dear God,

Thank you for being the author of my story and for knowing the best time to reveal the details for my story. I confess that I don't always live a life in display of my faith and trust in your timing of events in my life. Reveal to me the areas of doubt that I possess and am blind to. Open my eyes and provide me with opportunities to practice your commands, your word, and hospitality. Provide me with your strength that allows me to utilize all of the things you equipped me with to do your will. Thank you for setting me free from my slavery to sin and for gifting me with eternal life by means of Jesus and his sacrifice on the cross. I desire to live my life as a product of your influence, and not to fall under the influence of sin. I confess my perceived needs aren't always aligned with what the Bible says my needs are, and ask for you to supply me with your never-ending healing and mercy. Show me in what ways you want to use me to supply the needs of others as a reflection of my thankfulness toward you.

In Jesus' name,
Amen.

**CHAPTER SIX**

# I Am _____ Enough

## Lesson 1: Adequacy

Dating all the way back to our birth, we never had any trouble telling our parents when "enough was enough." The concept of what "enough" means is one we learn early on in life. This truth is likely the easiest of all of the truths in this book to both recognize and communicate, but I believe that inherently, we understand this truth the least.

Humans are excellent at measuring. For any measurement we take, some kind of "ruler" is used. When we measure by the incorrect ruler, what is actually enough and what we think is enough don't align. Even though our rulers almost always measure from an external perspective in the sense of us taking measurements of the world around us, for this chapter I'm going to reverse that focus to measuring what resides within us. How can we know that *we* are enough?

> **Enough:** *adjective* sufficient; in or to a degree or quantity that suffices: sufficiently; fully, quite[31]

The truth "I am _____ enough" looks vastly different depending on how we fill in that blank. However, in every case, this truth is based off of a comparison. This comparison possesses the ability to generate feelings of either "coming up short" or "being too much" depending on the nature of the situation.

---

31  *Merriam-Webster's Dictionary and Thesaurus,* Updated Edition, s.v. "Enough."

In this first lesson, we will address the concept of adequacy, as the word "adequately" is a synonym to the word "enough."[32] That said, our struggle to believe we are enough often stems from feelings of inadequacy. Whether it's from thinking that we're not good enough, smart enough, pretty enough, etc., something in our path has blinded us from seeing our adequacy. In what ways should we find our adequacy?

> **Adequate:** *adjective* equal to or sufficient for a specific requirement[33]

Adequacy results from knowing we have the tools necessary to carry out our certain purpose. When we think we possess *enough* of something to fulfill a requirement.

**When was a time where you *did* feel adequate for the requirement or purpose at hand?**

_____

_____

_____

_____

**When was a time where you *did not* feel adequate for the requirement or purpose at hand?**

_____

_____

_____

_____

---

32  *Merriam-Webster's Dictionary and Thesaurus,* Updated Edition, s.v. "Enough."
33  *Merriam-Webster's Dictionary and Thesaurus,* Updated Edition, s.v. "Adequate."

**Which of the above questions did you find easier to answer and why?**

_____

_____

_____

_____

My guess is, for most of us, coming up with a situation where we *did not* feel adequate was easier. For myself, feelings of inadequacy plagued the way that I pursued relationships of every type for years. Those feelings ruled my thoughts telling me, "Surely, my personality alone isn't enough to attract a guy in the timing I desire. Who's attracted to the science nerd?" and "Where will my looks ever get me? I am nowhere near the level of 'girly' in comparison to most women." Thoughts of my inadequacy began to drive my behavior, so in order to get the meaningful relationship I desired, I competed. I worked myself to the point where I partied so often, reaching for the bottle was second nature. I gained a drinking tolerance unmatched by almost every other person my size that I hung around. As I fed off of the equally competitive nature of those around me, I gained respect. At last, I found myself "adequate enough" to deserve attention.

I got so good at gaining favor from those around me that the people of the particular school I partied with often knighted me an official member of their crew and called me their "honorary engineer." In my view of adequacy, my natural self wasn't enough. I gained my adequacy by consuming unhealthy amounts of alcohol. Thankfully, the Bible portrays a significantly different viewpoint of what it means to be adequate. In the following passage, we see an example of the difference between our definition of what's necessary and Jesus's definition of what's necessary:

> *The apostles came back and told Jesus everything they had done. He took them with him, and they went off by themselves to a town named Bethsaida. When the crowds heard about it, they followed him. He welcomed them, spoke to them about the Kingdom of God, and healed those who needed it. When the sun was beginning to set, the twelve disciples came to him*

*and said, "Send the people away so that they can go to the villages and farms around here and find food and lodging, because this is a lonely place." But Jesus said to them, "You yourselves give them something to eat." They answered, "All we have are five loaves and two fish. Do you want us to go and buy food for this whole crowd?" (There were about five thousand men there.) Jesus said to his disciples, "Make the people sit down in groups of about fifty each." After the disciples had done so, Jesus took the five loaves and two fish, looked up to heaven, thanked God for them, broke them, and gave them to the disciples to distribute to the people. They all ate and had enough, and the disciples took up twelve baskets of what was left over. Luke 9:10-17*

In this passage, both the human definition of adequacy and the Godly definition of adequacy play out. What the disciples saw as inadequate, Jesus saw as adequate. How did both Jesus and the disciples respond differently to the same situation? When the disciples saw the five loaves and two fish meant to feed a crowd of five thousand men, they responded with, "Do you want us to go buy food for this whole crowd?" When Jesus saw the five loaves and two fish to feed a crowd of five thousand men, he "took the five loaves and two fish, looked up to heaven, thanked God for them, broke them, and gave them to the disciples to distribute to the people."

Looking at this story from the human perspective, we can easily see why we often struggle to believe the truth "I am _____ enough." There is *no way* those disciples could bear the leftover cost necessary to feed the crowd of five thousand men that the original five loaves and two fish didn't satisfy.

Fixing our eyes upon God's vision and purpose means allowing God to give us everything we need for fulfillment. In the beginning of the passage, the disciples told Jesus to send the people elsewhere in order to find food because they were in a "lonely place." The disciples did not see Jesus's plan to feed the crowd of five thousand men present.

We often take the same viewpoint as the disciples when assessing situations. We see the situation playing out before us, look around at the resources by our side, and determine whether or not the task at hand can be accomplished. Rather than looking to our perfect Father and using the Spirit he gives us for provision, we deem the situation as impossible and seek to abort the mission permanently.

As I searched for relationships, instead of turning to God and thanking him for all of the gifts I did have, all I saw was every one of my "inadequacies." No matter how "small" we picture the resources God supplies us with, he is capable of multiplying our resources to exceed what is necessary for any purpose he lays on our path.

**Have you ever found yourself trying to be like the disciples and providing God with solutions to a situation before seeking his perspective first? What was the result of that situation?**

_____

_____

_____

**Look back on a situation where you did not feel adequate, are you able to see how God provided your needs along the way?**

_____

_____

_____

**Are there any areas where you currently do not feel adequate? How can you take your situation and look at it with the perspective Jesus had in that passage and look to God for provision?**

_____

_____

_____

_____

## Lesson 2: Sufficiency

What if I said every single one of us, just for the sole reason of existing, will enable something to occur in this world that wouldn't have occurred otherwise? Every one of our stories matters, but the depression and anxiety driven culture swarming around us attempts to say otherwise. With technology, the increased visibility our society now has allows us to compare ourselves on a greater level than ever before. We see everything people accomplish and wonder why we aren't there too. We hear messages such as, "I don't matter." "Society doesn't need me." and "Someone else would do this better than I would." Every one of those messages prevents us from recognizing the fact we are enough.

Looking into one of the definitions of "enough" we simply see the word "sufficient."[34]

> **Sufficient:** *adjective* adequate to accomplish a purpose or meet a need[35]

The feeling of being enough in this sense requires us to first know our purpose. However, seeing our purpose itself is only half of the story. We must also believe that we are sufficiently equipped to accomplish our purpose. How can we be assured of our own sufficiency for our purpose? A truth we must understand in conjunction with believing we are enough, is that God created each of us for a purpose.

> *But I have raised you up for this very purpose, that I might show you my power and that my name might be proclaimed in all the earth. Exodus 9:16 NIV*

**What does the statement "God has created you for a purpose" mean to you?**

_____

_____

_____

_____

---

34    *Merriam-Webster's Dictionary and Thesaurus,* Updated Edition, s.v. "Enough."
35    *Merriam-Webster's Dictionary and Thesaurus,* Updated Edition, s.v. "Sufficient."

The verse in Exodus states our purpose is dually faceted: to allow God to show us his power and to proclaim his name across the earth.

Let's first look at the aspect of God's power. How does God show us his power? If at any time in our life we pray to receive Christ, we receive the gift of God's Holy Spirit. With this Spirit, we are filled with power.

*For the Spirit God gave us does not make us timid, but gives us power, love and self-discipline. 2 Timothy 1:7 NIV*

When each of us prays to receive the Holy Spirit, we not only receive God's power, but also spiritual gifts. God gives us these spiritual gifts to assist with fulfilling his purpose for us here on earth.

*There are different kinds of spiritual gifts, but the same Spirit gives them. There are different ways of serving, but the same Lord is served. There are different abilities to perform service, but the same God gives ability to all for their particular service. The Spirit's presence is shown in some way in each person for the good of all. 1 Corinthians 12:4-7*

God creates a specific purpose for every single person. We are the *only* one sufficient enough to carry out how that purpose looks using the unique set of spiritual gifts given to us. When we do not carry out our purpose using those gifts, it decreases the effectiveness of the body of Christ as a whole. Continuing on in 1 Corinthians chapter 12, we see how that effect takes shape:

*Christ is like a single body, which has many parts; it is still one body, even though it is made up of different parts. In the same way, all of us, whether Jews or Gentiles, whether slaves or free, have been baptized into the one body by the same Spirit, and we have all been given the one Spirit to drink. For the body itself is not made up of only one part, but of many parts. If the foot were to say, "Because I am not a hand, I don't belong to the body," that would not keep it from being a part of the body. 1 Corinthians 12:12-15*

Often times when we don't see our own sufficiency, it's because we lose sight of our God-given purpose. I have learned part of my purpose here on earth is to be a light to women by speaking the truth that results from a life of intimacy in relationship with Christ. My admittedly-stubborn self found that out by pursuing relationships in the wrong places. Finding out my purpose came at the cost of longing to find an identity with the wrong people and putting myself in all environments possible to get me there. I had classes with mostly men. I spoke to mostly men at parties. It all came at the cost of living a life filled with lies. I led myself away from Christ. I was convinced that I could find fulfillment elsewhere. The only thing partying really did was distract me from my true purpose. I was living a life rooted in lies. Believing those lies left me searching in the wrong places. I got drunk and communicated in an inebriated state with more people than I can count, and in every case, the only constant was my lack of fulfillment the next day.

The grace of God behind it all is as a result of going through the craziness, my sufficiency for carrying out my true purpose has done nothing but increase. Using my experiences I had in my personal search for purpose allows me to better speak truth to others going through the same situations, and to share with everyone who reads this book.

Unhealthy views of sufficiency are easy to come by when we compare ourselves to people with different purposes than ours. If our purpose is to be the hand of the body, we cannot compare ourselves to others around us who were designed to be a foot or some other part of the body. Hands will *always* feel insufficient to feet when they think their purpose is to walk, and feet will *always* feel insufficient to hands when they think their purpose is to write. To avoid feeling this way, we must be aware of our purpose and the gifts we've been given to fulfill that purpose.

**Have you ever thought about your own spiritual gifts and do you know what any of them are?**

_____

_____

_____

_____

**When was a time in which you felt insufficient?**

_____

_____

_____

_____

**What led you to that thought, was it from comparing yourselves to earthly things?**

_____

_____

_____

_____

When we receive the Holy Spirit, we are gifted a unique set of gifts and abilities in order to proclaim God's name in a way that no one else can. We are all unique parts of the same body, and when one part falls or becomes ill, it causes the others not to function as designed.

**Knowing that you share the responsibility for other parts of the body to work properly, how can you encourage those around you who are also a part of the same body and empower them to use the gifts God has given them?**

_____

_____

_____

_____

## Lesson 3: Measuring Up

Someone comes to us and asks, "What is the temperature outside?" Our answer to that question will likely come in the form of some number of "degrees." To determine how many degrees it is, a measurement of the environment outside must be taken. The weather conditions each day depend upon several variables. When the temperature is cold enough, snow falls instead of rain. When enough sun shines in the right places after a downpour, a rainbow forms. This concept of being enough leads to the definition, "in or to a degree or quantity that suffices."[36] When looking at the idea of measuring up in the context of our purpose, we find that the world constantly gives us standards to "measure up" against. How do we gauge our ability to measure up, and are we even measuring up to the proper criteria?

**Measure:** *noun* a basis or standard of comparison: criterion[37]

To experience and live in the fullness of the truth "I am _____ enough" we need to measure ourselves against healthy standards. The standards we choose to measure up and compare ourselves against can either be set by God or ourselves and other people.

**Have you ever found yourself setting your own standards? If so, what are they?**

_____

_____

_____

_____

**How do you find yourself measuring up with those standards?**

_____

_____

_____

_____

---

36  *Merriam-Webster's Dictionary and Thesaurus,* Updated Edition, s.v. "Enough."
37  *Merriam-Webster's Dictionary and Thesaurus,* Updated Edition, s.v. "Measure."

In order to we feel like we are enough, the standards we live by need to have achievable measurements.

The Bible discusses the results and the differences of living from both human standards and Godly standards. The emotions generated from both types of standards are drastically different. To decipher whether we are living by human standards or Godly standards, we must know the difference in those feelings. First, we will take a look at the results of living by human standards:

> **Judgment:** *"You judge by human standards; I pass judgment on no one." John 8:15 NIV*
>
> **Conformity:** *Do not conform yourselves to the standards of this world, but let God transform you inwardly by a complete change of your mind. Then you will be able to know the will of God—what is good and is pleasing to him and is perfect. Romans 12:2*
>
> **Foolishness:** *Brothers and sisters, think of what you were when you were called. Not many of you were wise by human standards; not many were influential; not many were of noble birth. 1 Corinthians 1:26 NIV*

The life that I created for myself as I searched for a meaningful relationship was completely rooted in human standards. I had standards that any guy I talked to needed to meet, one of those being the type of intimacy I was searching for. I never wanted a relationship based solely on physical intimacy, but rather a relational intimacy. Finding that type of relationship proved to be impossible. But, I'm the type of person who can do anything I put my mind to, so I kept trying.

My efforts shifted on one memorable night. It started out like any other regular night, I had plans to go out with a guy to a party. However, shortly before those plans were to happen, he cancelled on me and instead, I asked a different friend to go to a separate party. We found ourselves drunk and back home in the middle of the night to an alert that got sent area-wide. The alert was about the same guy I originally had plans to go out with.

I had never felt so foolish in my life. What if I had stuck with my original plans and that alert was about something that had happened to me? I had no idea what I needed to do, but I knew my environment needed to change.

Changing my environment was much easier said than done. Investing in the party lifestyle for much of the year leading up to that night, the people I partied with had formed unrealistic expectations of me. I needed to consume a certain amount of alcohol or I faced unspoken judgment. I didn't know how to achieve both my change of environment and stay in the same location, so I fled completely. I moved to pursue a new group of friends and made the decision that if I was going to continue the partying life, I was at least going to do it with friends that I had deeper relationships with, and not with people I had met one or two times before. My standards changed, but the way I pursued meeting those standards would remain the same.

**Describe a time where either you compared yourself or someone else compared you to human standards and it resulted in judgment, conformation, or foolishness?**

_____

_____

_____

_____

**How was the situation resolved? If it is still present, how can you invite God into that situation?**

_____

_____

_____

_____

The standards God sets for us have much different implications than human standards. When it comes to God's standards, we don't have to worry about measuring up to them. God sets achievable standards for everyone. He is a good Father, a perfect Creator, and would never create a standard to set us up for failure. The results from living by God's standards are:

**Freedom**: _But thanks be to God, that you who were once slaves of sin have become obedient from the heart to the standard of teach-_

*ing to which you were committed, and, having been set free from*
*sin, have become slaves of righteousness. Romans 6:17-18 ESV*
**Truth:** *Stop judging by external standards, and judge by true*
*standards. John 7:24*
**Equality:** *For God judges everyone by the same standard.*
*Romans 2:11*

The last verse from Romans tells us that God holds the same standards for everyone. With God's standards, we have nothing to measure up to with respect to any other person. We all belong on the same, level, playing field. When we realize our freedom from not living a life of slavery to our sin, we can live in the truth that we are enough.

When I set myself free from striving to live up to other people's unrealistic expectations for my life, I gained the ability to pursue the great gifts God had for me. Access to freedom is available to each of us when we make the daily choice to live a life honoring of God's standards and not our own.

**Describe a time when you experienced freedom as a result of judging yourself by God's standards, rather than your own?**

_____

_____

_____

_____

**What daily action can you take to prevent from falling into the influence of external standards?**

_____

_____

_____

_____

## Lesson 4: Fullness

It's a Friday night and we're at a friend's house. They invited us over for dinner and asked us what our favorite meal was. After finishing the main course they ask us, "Are you full or would you like more to eat?" If our answer is, "No, thank you, I'm full." odds are, we feel like we've had *enough* to eat. The last definition of "enough" that we will explore in this chapter is "fully, quite."[38] We can all relate to eating food and the experience of fullness. Our hunger reminds us every day of our need for food.

The concept of hunger and feeling full also occurs in a spiritual sense. How can we take a look at this concept of "enough" from a spiritual aspect? If Christ truly is enough for all of our needs, what does it look like to experience a fullness in Christ?

**What do you think a fullness in Christ looks like?**

_____

_____

_____

_____

Having the experience of being full comes as a result of reaching a point of satisfaction. From our satisfaction, the need to consume from other sources goes away. If we search for satisfaction in areas where God should be the source of fulfillment, the fullness we achieve is always temporal.

Even though my standards for who I drank with changed, the greater problem of seeking fulfillment from sources other than God remained. Whether I drank with people I'd never met before in my life, or with people I'd known for years, the same issues appeared. The drunkenness wore off in the morning, and to achieve the same state, I had to consume more alcohol.

Fulfillment from the things of this earth require an element of consumption. This consumption on one hand can be healthy. Consumption of food and water

---

38 *Merriam-Webster's Dictionary and Thesaurus,* Updated Edition, s.v. "Enough."

are necessary to prevent starvation or dehydration. Consumption can also be unhealthy, from the consumption of drugs, alcohol, porn, etc. What does consumption look like to God?

Unlike any earthly thing, where we are the only one who makes the choice to consume it, God makes the choice to consume us as well. Being consumed by God is as simple as inviting him into our lives and receiving the Holy Spirit. The moment we receive his Spirit, it remains with us. If we allow it, the Spirit consumes us. We don't have to re-ask for God's Spirit to get its fullness back the next day. As described in the following verse from Hebrews, God is a consuming fire.

> *Therefore, since we are receiving a kingdom that cannot be shaken, let us be thankful, and so worship God acceptably with reverence and awe, for our "God is a consuming fire." Hebrews 12:28-29 NIV*

In God fullness exists. If we allow God to fill us, we don't have to reach to worldly sources to fill those same needs. The Bible describes God as a fullness of:

> **Grace**: *The Word became flesh and made his dwelling among us. We have seen his glory, the glory of the one and only Son, who came from the Father, full of grace and truth. John 1:14 NIV*
> **Joy**: *You make known to me the path of life; in your presence there is fullness of joy; at your right hand are pleasures forevermore. Psalm 16:11 ESV*
> **Knowledge**: *For now we see in a mirror dimly, but then face to face. Now I know in part; then I shall know fully, even as I have been fully known. 1 Corinthians 13:12 ESV*

**How have you experienced a fullness in Christ in the forms of grace, joy, or knowledge?**

_____

_____

_____

_____

In order to be filled in any capacity, we must first contain room with which to be filled. We can't experience God's fullness if we continually attempt to fill ourselves. In order to receive the fullness God has for us, we must empty ourselves first.

**What does it mean to empty yourself?**

_____

_____

_____

_____

**Empty:** *adjective* containing nothing[39]

Jesus is the only person to walk this earth who lived a life of emptiness unto himself and a fullness in God. He accomplished this by making himself nothing. Everything Jesus contained during his life on earth came from God, but how did he do it?

> In your relationships with one another, have the same mindset as Christ Jesus: Who, being in very nature God, did not consider equality with God something to be used to his own advantage; rather, he made himself nothing by taking the very nature of a servant, being made in human likeness. And being found in appearance as a man, he humbled himself by becoming obedient to death—even death on a cross! Philippians 2:5-8 NIV

This passage lays out several components for how to successfully empty ourselves. We must take on the attributes of servanthood, humbleness, and obedience. A quality each of those components share is the requirement for us to place someone or something else above or before ourselves. The "someone" in this case of the Philippians passage is God.

There's a reason why Philippians 4:13 is arguably the most popular verse in the entire book of Philippians. The concept of *I can do all things through him who strengthens me. ESV* comes across as more appealing, positive, and uplifting than the passage from Philippians 2. However, if we don't first submit to

---

39   *Merriam-Webster's Dictionary and Thesaurus,* Updated Edition, s.v. "Empty."

the command of Philippians 2 and make ourselves nothing, we become incapable of fully receiving the strength spoken of in Philippians 4:13.

Philippians 2 is hard to swallow because the nature of the verses are the exact opposite of what our sinful nature deems as the rewarding thing to do. Since we know that God never leads us in the direction of disappointment, what makes emptying us of ourselves worth it? What kind of reward does a fullness in Christ bring?

> **Hope:** *May the God of hope fill you with all joy and peace as you trust in him, so that you may overflow with hope by the power of the Holy Spirit. Romans 15:13 NIV*
>
> **Wisdom:** *...that their hearts may be encouraged, being knit together in love, to reach all the riches of full assurance of understanding and the knowledge of God's mystery, which is Christ, in whom are hidden all the treasures of wisdom and knowledge. Colossians 2:2-3 ESV*
>
> **Boldness:** *After they prayed, the place where they were meeting was shaken. And they were all filled with the Holy Spirit and spoke the word of God boldly. Acts 4:31 NIV*

**What obstacles prevent you from being able to empty yourself?**

_____

_____

_____

**What feelings do you experience as a result of filling yourself with earthly desires?**

_____

_____

_____

_____

**How do those feelings differ from the things we can feel from a fullness in Christ?**

_____

_____

_____

_____

Dear God,

Renew my mind on what it means to be enough. Take away my fear of inadequacy, insufficiency, or emptiness in any situation. Give me your eyes to see what you provide for me in the areas where I don't feel like I possess as much as needed to get the job done. Thank you for being a God who creates each person for a specific purpose, including myself. Thank you for gifting me with a unique set of spiritual gifts that are sufficient enough to fulfill the purpose you created me for at all times. Give me your ears to hear your thoughts about me—thoughts based off of your judgment of me and not of human judgment, thoughts rooted in your standards resulting in freedom and not any human standards resulting in guilt. I confess I often do not live in a complete fullness in you. I ask for your grace, knowledge, and joy to be present in any areas of my life where I am lacking. I desire to live my life as a display of an emptiness to myself and of a fullness in you. Fill my life with your hope, wisdom, and boldness to overcome any attacks the enemy tries to throw my way.

In Jesus' name,
Amen.

## CHAPTER SEVEN

# I Am Smart

## Lesson 1: Quick in Action

t was a clear summer day in Ohio when my elementary-aged self ran around the house getting ready for a softball game. My running came to a halt after the door frame of my parent's bedroom greeted my forehead. The collision sent me to the floor, but somehow I felt no pain, so I picked myself up and proceeded to run around the house some more. As I made my way downstairs, blood began to drip onto my shirt. Panicking, I looked at my forehead and saw a gash prominent enough to warrant stitches. The worst part? I wasn't allowed to play in my softball game because I couldn't wear the hat from my uniform. Now, it doesn't take a genius to figure out that running around the house wasn't a particularly *smart* action on my part—I knew better. Regardless, I went against the will of my parents and did it anyway.

Possessing smartness goes far beyond how much we know, it also includes how we respond to what we know. Similar in nature to the truth "I am creative" our world likes to place stereotypes on what smartness looks like. People who are typically viewed as smart often belong to specific fields of study. The world loves to promote placing the "smart" kids in Science, Technology, Engineering, and Mathematics (STEM) fields. This perception creates a stigma that certain people are smarter than others. Satan loves the division this stigma creates, as it makes us an easy target for him to steer us away from the truth.

As a math and science tutor for many years, I have watched too many people, both children and adults, struggle to believe the truth that they are smart. Almost all of their struggle either comes from comparing themselves to others in their classes, or perceiving the quantity of knowledge they possess as being far less than what they think they should have. The word "smart" wears multiple different hats in the English language, possessing smartness goes beyond equating our smartness to our quantity of knowledge.

**Smart:** *adjective* quick or prompt in action, as persons; having or showing quick intelligence or ready mental capability; shrewd or sharp, as a person in dealing with others or as in business dealings; socially elegant; sophisticated or fashionable; clever, witty, or readily effective, as a speaker, speech, rejoinder, etc.[40]

Rather than focusing on academics, this chapter will dig deeper into how to become smart with our faith, starting with how we can be people who are quick to act on our faith. From a knowledge context, this may look like people quickly getting the right answers to questions. How does this component of the definition of smart change when talking on the subject of our faith?

**Think of a time in which you quickly acted on your faith. What was the result?**

_____

_____

_____

_____

As Christians, one of the smartest decisions we can make is to live a life in which all of our actions are prompted by our faith. Acting on our faith requires us to say "yes" to God and "no" to ourselves. The quicker we say "yes" to God, the sooner we step onto the path God creates for us. The enemy hates when we are on the path God created for us. To fight back, he attempts to bring us down in the midst of those actions. This "bringing down" commonly shows up in two forms:

---

40  *Dictionary.com,* s.v. "Smart," accessed November 1, 2018, https://www.dictionary.com/

**Fear:** *There is no fear in love. But perfect love drives out fear, because fear has to do with punishment. The one who fears is not made perfect in love. 1 John 4:18 NIV*
**Anxiety:** *Anxiety in a man's heart weighs him down, but a good word makes him glad. Proverbs 12:25 ESV*

**How do fear or anxiety prevent you from acting out in faith?**

_____

_____

_____

_____

**How did you overcome any previous fear or anxiety to take a step of faith?**

_____

_____

_____

_____

Making the decision to take a step of faith is often difficult. The results of our stepping out in faith are often unknown. If the results are unknown, how can we know that taking a step of faith is worth it? The Bible states that our faith becomes *perfected* by our actions, not hindered by them.

*So it is with faith: if it is alone and includes no actions, then it is dead. But someone will say, "One person has faith, another has actions." My answer is, "Show me how anyone can have faith without actions. I will show you my faith by my actions." Do you believe that there is only one God? Good! The demons also believe—and tremble with fear. You fool! Do you want to be shown that faith without actions is useless? How was our ances-*

*tor Abraham put right with God? It was through his actions, when he offered his son Isaac on the altar. Can't you see? His faith and his actions worked together; his faith was made perfect through his actions. James 2:17-22*

We bring our faith to life by acting upon it. Our life is defined by any object we place our faith in, not just God. For that reason, identifying where we place our faith is crucial.

Shortly after the night when the alert was sent out, I made the decision to pack my bags and move. I went back to a familiar place that was nearer to people I had long-standing relationships with. Regardless of the fact that none of those relationships were as relationally intimate as I craved, I placed my faith in my ability to deepen them when I arrived. The best part? I didn't have to change my drinking habits in my attempt to accomplish this task. As far as I was concerned, my plan was unstoppable.

I placed my faith in the perception that the environment I moved to would be more conducive for facilitating the relationship I wanted. Eventually, I would find what I was looking for. Looking at my move based solely on a relationship component, I made a really *smart* choice. However, those relationships were not found in the people, places, or timing upon which I made the decision to move.

From a faith perspective, I made an unintelligent decision. I placed my faith in my ability to meet and interact with the people I deemed as being the "right" people, on nothing but my own judgment. I had zero faith in God's ability to move me in the direction he wanted me to go or in his ability to bring people capable of providing life-giving relationships into my life. Thankfully, God's will is always done, he is always faithful, and the relationships with the people he led me to were what would eventually drive me back into the most important relationship—a relationship with Jesus.

**In what ways is God calling you to act out on your faith?**

_____

_____

_____

_____

**How can you ask God to assist you in being prompt with those callings?**

_____

_____

_____

_____

〰〰〰

## Lesson 2: Readiness

Before reading this lesson, I want to encourage everyone to take a moment to sit with God in preparation. We all have areas God prepares us in as we live out our story.

**What does God want you to be ready for?**

_____

_____

_____

_____

In the definition, "having or showing quick intelligence or ready mental capability,"[41] it mentions the concept of readiness. People often earn the perception of intelligence based on their performance on tests. In order to consistently perform well on tests, preparation beforehand is critical. Preparation looks vastly different for each person, but when we faithfully execute our preparation, our readiness for any test life throws at us increases. One of the primary reasons some people test higher than others is because the level of preparation they put in beforehand is greater.

---

41   *Dictionary.com,* s.v. "Smart," accessed November 1, 2018, https://www.dictionary.com/

Nowhere in this aspect of "smart" do we see a reference to a quantity of knowledge. It refers to both the speed of our response in times of testing, and how ready or prepared we were to respond. We've all taken more tests than we care to admit in our lives. The more prepared we are for the test, the quicker we are able to answer the questions, and the better we perform. Does this same concept carry any relevance when translated to a faith-based perspective?

> *Count it all joy, my brothers, when you meet trials of various kinds, for you know that the testing of your faith produces steadfastness. And let steadfastness have its full effect, that you may be perfect and complete, lacking in nothing. James 1:2-4 ESV*

**How has your faith recently been tested?**

_____

_____

_____

_____

**What resulted from those tests and did you feel more complete as a result?**

_____

_____

_____

_____

A key word from the passage in James is the word *when*. Trials of various kinds are bound to come our way. It isn't a matter of if, but when. The type of faith referred to in the passage is a faith in God. However, we experience the same kind of testing with anything we place our faith in.

When I decided to move, I placed a very high level of faith in my new environment to provide me with satisfying and fulfilling relationships. Now, don't get me wrong, I made many great friends then that I still hold dear to this day. Both acquiring and maintaining friends was never the problem—my problem was that I placed a God-sized faith in something other than God.

The truth is, it never mattered where I lived or who I hung out with. No place or person on this earth will ever provide any one of us with a relationship as satisfying and fulfilling as a relationship with God. Although my example is just one, this truth remains for anything we place our faith in outside of God.

Why is having a relationship with God so much more fulfilling? In the passage from James, it says, "the testing of your faith produces steadfastness." The word "steadfast" simply means "not subject to change."[42] The only "not changing" variable on this earth is change itself. Change is inevitable. Our relationships, places, and circumstances constantly change. The only source qualified to produce unchanging, steadfast results is God.

*Jesus Christ is the same yesterday and today and forever.*
*Hebrews 13:8 NIV*

By placing my faith in myself to facilitate relationships, the results were anything but steadfast. My results were conditional upon my ability to perform. That ability changed on a nightly basis dependent upon any number of external factors influencing my ability to drink.

God on the other hand, never changes. His love for us is steadfast, his care for us is steadfast, and nothing we ever do will influence his opinion of us. The only thing we need to have is faith in his steadfastness.

How can we be smart in our faith and also be ready for the trials ahead of us? The following passage displays qualities for a readiness in our faith.

*So then, have your minds ready for action. Keep alert and set your hope completely on the blessing which will be given you when Jesus Christ is revealed. Be obedient to God, and do not allow your lives to be shaped by those desires you had while you were still ignorant. Instead, be holy in all that you do, just as God who called you is holy. The scripture says, "Be holy because I am holy." You call him Father, when you pray to God, who judges all people by the same standard, according to what each one has done; so then, spend the rest of your lives here*

---

42    *Merriam-Webster's Dictionary and Thesaurus,* Updated Edition, s.v. "Steadfast."

*on earth in reverence for him. For you know what was paid to set you free from the worthless manner of life handed down by your ancestors. It was not something that can be destroyed, such as silver or gold; it was the costly sacrifice of Christ, who was like a lamb without defect or flaw. He had been chosen by God before the creation of the world and was revealed in these last days for your sake. Through him you believe in God, who raised him from death and gave him glory; and so your faith and hope are fixed on God. 1 Peter 1:13-21*

A readiness in our faith includes: alertness, hope, obedience, and living by God's desires. Three of the four pieces of equipment refer to where we are to place our faith, in God. The fourth piece is the need to be alert, or in other words, ready and prepared. If we take these elements into consideration during our next test of faith, we will become more ready, or smarter, in the way we respond to that test.

**How can you better prepare for your own next test in faith?**

_____

_____

_____

_____

**Are there any tests of faith you have overcome more quickly now as a result of learning from past tests? What are they and what enables you to be quicker in your response?**

_____

_____

_____

_____

## Lesson 3: Sharpness

We've been sent to the nearest thrift store on a last-minute quest to buy a set of steak knives. Perusing section of utensils, we encounter two equally priced options: a set of dull, name-brand steak knives and a set of sharp, off-brand steak knives. With limited time to make a decision, which set do we choose? Assuming we don't conveniently have a knife sharpener at home, we're going to pick the set capable of cutting steak immediately: the sharp set.

Just like knives can be sharp or dull, our minds possess that same ability. Although, what it means for a knife to be sharp and what it means for our minds to be sharp looks different, the concepts of sharpness and retaining sharpness apply to both. We see people as intellectually sharp when they come up with solutions to problems in clever ways, likely in ways the others who worked on the same issue did not see. How can we also apply this concept of being sharp to our faith?

Any object that can possess sharpness becomes dull over time after repeated use. People are no different, and God uses us as an instrument to sharpen one another.

*As iron sharpens iron, so one person sharpens another. Proverbs 27:17 NIV*

**What do you think it means to be a person who sharpens others?**

_____

_____

_____

_____

What does it look like for us to sharpen one another? How do we stay sharp ourselves? Similar in nature to our physical bodies needing exercise, our faith is to be exercised as well. If we continually exercise our faith and do not make it a habit to go back to the source that our faith is rooted in, we become exhausted. We require sharpening of some kind to sustainably exercise our faith. To live a life in accordance to the Bible and its truth, we are the objects both being sharpened and the tool that is sharpening those around us. We can't sharpen others unless we are sharp ourselves first. Our faith is sharpened by spending time in the Bible.

> For the word of God is alive and active. Sharper than any dou-
> ble-edged sword, it penetrates even to dividing soul and spirit,
> joints and marrow; it judges the thoughts and attitudes of the
> heart. Hebrews 4:12 NIV

**Do you ever face challenges in spending consistent time in the Bible? If so, what are the reasons or causes for those challenges? If not, how did you get to that point?**

_____

_____

_____

_____

Keeping the verse from Hebrews in mind, we can reason that spending time in God's word sharpens us. What can we anticipate from living a life according to the Bible?

> Keep this Book of the Law always on your lips; meditate on
> it day and night, so that you may be careful to do everything
> written in it. Then you will be prosperous and successful.
> Joshua 1:8 NIV

The passage in Joshua tells us that when we take the time to live out God's word, we become both successful and prosperous. Meditating on the word of God maintains smartness. However, a knowledge of the Bible must be paired with a faith in Jesus, the Law alone does not impart life. Jesus lived his life on earth as a fulfillment of the Law, and those of us who call ourselves believers gain eternal life as a result of placing our faith in Jesus.

> For if the inheritance depends on the law, then it no longer
> depends on the promise; but God in his grace gave it to Abra-
> ham through a promise. Why, then, was the law given at all? It

*was added because of transgressions until the Seed to whom the promise referred had come. The law was given through angels and entrusted to a mediator. A mediator, however, implies more than one party; but God is one. Is the law, therefore, opposed to the promises of God? Absolutely not! For if a law had been given that could impart life, then righteousness would certainly have come by the law. But Scripture has locked up everything under the control of sin, so that what was promised, being given through faith in Jesus Christ, might be given to those who believe. Galatians 3:18-22 NIV*

The amount of faith that we possess to some degree correlates with the amount of time we spend in the word and getting to know God's character. We can't put our faith in anything unless we believe in it first, and we can't place belief in anything we've never heard of before. The more we know about a topic, the more confidently we can place our belief in it. Spending time in God's word allows us to learn about his character and how to live in a life-giving way rather than a life-taking way centered on both the world's expectations and our own expectations for us.

As I sought to find validation in relationships from everyone other than God, I quickly drifted away from spending any time in the Bible. The friendships I had were significantly more fulfilling than most of the ones I moved away from. I could trust that I would party with them on a consistent basis. I didn't think I had to drink to a certain capacity to impress them, but I did anyway because drinking was too much a part of my identity not to give it my best by this point. Along with the increase in my fulfillment came an increase in the frequency of the times I drank. Who needed to spend time in the Bible when life was going so well?

I didn't have a strong enough foundation built on my faith during childhood to believe spending time in the Bible had any worth. When I went to college, I left my Bible behind at my parent's house and allowed it to collect dust in their closet. This caused me to drift further and further away from God until he placed someone in my life who was sharp in his word. That person recognized their role to sharpen others, saw my own lack of sharpness, and began to encourage me to spend time in the Bible. Not only did they seek to bring light into my lack of sharpness, they didn't expect me to have to sharpen them in return. They understood the role the Bible plays in sharpening them first.

It's not always the easiest route to take, but if we truly believe God is as good as he claims, walking down the path he creates for us will never lead us astray. In addition, if anything we ever hear contradicts with the Bible, steer clear of the path quickly. That path is not from God!

**How has success resulted in your life by living a life aligned with God's word?**

_____

_____

_____

_____

**How has your faith in God strengthened as a result of a greater knowledge of God's character?**

_____

_____

_____

_____

**How can you show the importance of, encourage, and sharpen those around you, encouraging them to spend more time in the word?**

_____

_____

_____

_____

## Lesson 4: Elegance

We're walking into a ballroom style wedding reception. We see a room full of women in long flowing dresses and men in black suits and bow ties. The tables are set with fine china and crystal stemware, and chandeliers hang from the ceiling. A symphony plays music off to the side as we watch couples enter the dance floor.

It would be easy for someone to enter this reception and become taken back by the elegance of the surroundings. In reality, this wedding contains elements no different from any other wedding where we would get dressed up, eat food, hear music, and dance.

The concept of elegance is not only presented in physical aspects, but also in social aspects. In the list of definitions for "smart" is the phrase "socially elegant."[43] With this definition, we see again how it is not about the actual amount of what we know about a subject, but rather how we present what we know. I'm sure that almost every one of us has listened to someone speak and thought to ourselves, "That person sounds really smart." Chances are, we become more willing to believe that what a person has to say is fact when we have those thoughts about them. We allot a larger amount of our time and attention to listen to them speak.

When we receive the time and attention from others as a result of social elegance, we must be good stewards of their time. Depending on the subject at hand, the result of our conversations will quickly veer off in the directions of either being life-giving or life-taking.

The more comfortable I became in social settings, the more I became a master of life-taking social elegance. I perfected my gift for talking with and relating to others during my summer of doing door-to-door sales where I obtained great practice in speaking to multiple different types of audiences daily. Door-to-door sales presented a platform where even if I failed to relate with one customer, a list of new houses with opportunities to get it right was at my fingertips. Unlike my childhood where I was surrounded with insecurities of people wanting to spend the time to talk with me, my fear of rejection was removed and I eventually perfected the art of relating to customers.

I then translated those skills into my everyday friendships. Because of my foundation of good friends, making new ones was less risky. Everyone I came

---

43   *Dictionary.com,* s.v. "Smart," accessed November 1, 2018, https://www.dictionary.com/

into contact with became a potential friend. Rather than approaching someone and saying, "Hi, my name is Emily. I'm going around your neighborhood helping people meet the demand of their cable and internet needs." My conversations were, "Hi, my name is Emily, you're friends with _____? How do you know them? What are you studying?" The conversations seem simple, but both worked well. It's not a secret, people love talking about themselves for the most part. If we show them our interest, they will likely talk. At the core, these conversations held much life-giving potential.

The problem was, I centered those conversations on life-taking activities. Making a greater number of friends around life-taking activities only sent me deeper down a life-taking path. I was rarely concerned with having nothing to do on Saturday night. I had plenty of friends I could reach out to and find the location of the next big party. I constantly surrounded myself in these party environments that distracted me from pursuing a relationship with God. The better I became at figuring out how to adapt and relate myself in those environments, the less I cared to be anywhere else.

It came to a point where I decided I didn't need God, and my faith took a hit because of it. My desire for an intimate relationship remained, but I figured all I had to do was meet the right person and all would be cured. I had no way of knowing how to get out of that mindset until someone took a chance at sharing their faith with me. Their elegance in the way they spoke to me caused me to give them more time to do so. Their social elegance was life-giving.

We all possess the ability to be socially elegant in sharing our faith, but how? For starters, we have to be willing to speak up about our faith. The Bible is very clear in calling all of us who identify as followers of Christ to be sharers of the good news to others.

> He said to them, "Go throughout the whole world and preach the gospel to all people. Whoever believes and is baptized will be saved; whoever does not believe will be condemned." Mark 16:15-16

**What do you commonly feel when bringing up your faith with others? How do those feelings change depending on the person you're talking with?**

_____

_____

_____

_____

**What barriers do you face when vocalizing your faith for the first time with a person? Do those barriers change when it's with someone you just met versus someone you've known for years?**

_____

_____

_____

_____

Not only is it important for us to vocalize our faith, we need to also be careful in how we share it. What does a social elegance in sharing our faith look like? A couple of synonyms to the word "elegance" are "class" and "grace."[44] When we share our faith with others, we must not do so in an offensive way, but rather by showing grace to all we share with.

> ...*but in your hearts regard Christ the Lord as holy, always being prepared to make a defense to anyone who asks you for a reason for the hope that is in you; yet do it with gentleness and respect, having a good conscience, so that, when you are slandered, those who revile your good behavior in Christ may be put to shame. 1 Peter 3:15-16 ESV*

When we truly recognize the amount of grace God extends to us, sharing our faith to others by means of gentleness and grace becomes second nature.

As a result of recognizing this for myself, I learned to be socially elegant in a life-giving way. God redeemed my story, and I became a better steward of his gifts to me. Now when I approach new people, I use my gift of getting to know them and my desire to help them in a life-giving manner. Instead of bringing people into a life filled with drinking and partying, I invite them to join me in discovering a life driven by following Jesus. I stop at nothing to share my faith with as many people as possible, whether it's with a stranger

---

44  *Merriam-Webster's Dictionary and Thesaurus,* Updated Edition, s.v. "Elegance."

along the street, with others in small groups I lead, or in this book. My hope is in Jesus because *no one else* will ever step foot on this planet who loves us more than he does.

**What is the reason for the hope that is within you?**

_____

_____

_____

_____

**In what ways or areas do you feel unprepared to defend the reason for the hope that is within you?**

_____

_____

_____

_____

**Is there anyone in your circle of influence who you should gracefully share where your hope comes from? How can you ask God to help you approach them?**

_____

_____

_____

_____

## Lesson 5: Effectiveness

Imagine a group of people in a room where everyone is posed with the same challenge. They are each instructed to build a tower as tall as possible, with one restriction; a time limit. Everyone in the room would complete the challenge, but not everyone would complete the challenge in the same way. If someone built a tower that stood five feet, and another that stood five inches, would we perceive the one who built the five-foot tower as smarter? If we looked at their effectiveness to complete the challenge in the variable of height alone, we might be right. However, if the one who built the five-foot tower did so because they had access to bricks, and the other who built the tower of five inches did so because had access to feathers, did either of them more effectively complete the challenge? I would say "no," they were both equally effective at completing the challenge with the resources they had access to.

The last definition of "smart" we will address is to be "readily effective."[45] Just as we saw effectiveness in a couple of aspects in the example of the tower building, we also have the ability to be effective with our faith. What does being effective in our faith look like?

**Effective:** *adjective* actually in operation or in force; functioning[46]

The primary word in the definition of effective I want to focus on is "force." In the world of physics, the force of an object equals the mass of that object multiplied by its acceleration. Meaning, anything with force must have two components: weight and motion.

Good or bad, it is up to us to determine which forces we allow to impact our free will and our lives. The force of relationships in my new home appeared to be continuing in a positive direction. I had meaningful, long-standing friends, the confidence to make new friends, and no sign of any forces stopping my life satisfaction from continuing to grow anytime soon. Or at least that's what I saw.

Because of my unwillingness to surrender my relationships to a God I had little faith in, I forced myself to go through the motions and carry out my success. This logic appeared to be easy, because it required no faith in Jesus at all, but rather a faith in my own ability to maintain my circumstances. Although

---

45  *Dictionary.com*, s.v. "Smart," accessed November 1, 2018, https://www.dictionary.com/

46  *Dictionary.com*, s.v. "Effective," accessed November 1, 2018, https://www.dictionary.com/

things at the time were going well, I'm not God. It would only be a matter of time before the weight of my own success would crush me.

**What currently weighs you down and how does it prevent you from moving in your faith?**

_____

_____

_____

_____

The larger the amount of weight we allow our faith to possess in our lives, the more faith can move us, and the greater the amount of force our faith carries. The more force faith carries in our life, the more effective we become in living a life based in our faith. Just how much movement can living out a faith in Jesus cause? We see a glimpse of how much in the following parable of Jesus healing a demon-possessed boy:

> *Jesus rebuked the demon, and it came out of the boy, and he was healed at that moment. Then the disciples came to Jesus in private and asked, "Why couldn't we drive it out?" He replied, "Because you have so little faith. Truly I tell you, if you have faith as small as a mustard seed, you can say to this mountain, 'Move from here to there,' and it will move. Nothing will be impossible for you." Matthew 17:18-20 NIV*

When we have faith even as small as the size of a mustard seed, we are capable of moving mountains. Even more important than moving mountains, our faith can be an example to how others can find the same movement within themselves.

> *I always thank my God as I remember you in my prayers, because I hear about your love for all his holy people and your faith in the Lord Jesus. I pray that your partnership with us in the faith may be effective in deepening your understanding of every good thing we share for the sake of Christ. Your love has given me great joy and encouragement, because you,*

*brother, have refreshed the hearts of the Lord's people. Phile-*
*mon 1:4-7 NIV*

As I increased the amount of faith in myself to build the relationships I desired, the mountain surrounding my heart became both larger and harder to move. The amount of effort required for me to pour out and sustain the lifestyle that I created was beginning to become insurmountable. The problem was, nothing I placed my faith in was capable of moving it. Nothing would ever move this mountain until I could get myself to a point where I realized I didn't need to have my life figured out.

The truth is, we don't need to have everything figured out. Jesus wants a relationship with each of us regardless of whether we have things figured out or not. Understanding how much God wants a relationship with us, and helping others to find the same for themselves, is the smartest and most effective way to both grow in our own faith and share our faith with others.

**How has your faith deepened your understanding of God's goodness?**

_____

_____

_____

_____

**How have you seen love refresh the hearts of the Lord's people as a result of either you or someone you know acting out in faith?**

_____

_____

_____

_____

**How has your own heart been refreshed from people acting out in faith toward you? How were you motivated in your own faith because of it?**

_____

_____

_____

_____

Dear God,

I desire to live a life where my faith in you prompts all of my actions. I pray against any fear or anxiety in my life preventing me from moving in the direction you want me to go. Help me to see how my faith is made perfect in my actions, and to recognize the fear that is stopping me from completing those actions. I pray for an increased knowledge of how these acts of faith equip me to live the life you called me to, and how to use that equipment for entering future tests of faith that will come my way. Show me how to use the same equipment to sharpen those around me. Supply me with the peace and patience to help communicate my faith to others in a socially elegant way so I may have the gentleness necessary for sharpening others. I confess that I don't always live a life with a faith that is capable of moving any mountain in my path. I ask for you to lift the weight preventing me from moving freely in the hope you provide, and I pray against any of the enemy's attempts to slow down my effectiveness of walking on this path you set for me.

In Jesus' name,
Amen.

## CHAPTER EIGHT

# I Have a Purpose

## Lesson 1: Reason for Existence

It's a question all of us ask ourselves at some point in life. What are we doing on this earth? None of us asked for our existence, yet here we are. At some point, we all want to know why. I'm not preaching anything new when I say that life on earth isn't easy. We all have trials thrown our way, obstacles to overcome, and wonder along the way if it's all worth it in the end. It is by no means impossible to go through trials in life without knowing the purpose behind them, but when we see their purpose, we can live differently—obstacles become more bearable, we step into trials with greater authority, and having hope for what is to come is easier.

The truth "I have a purpose" takes the "I am useful" truth to a deeper level. It's one thing to know we are useful, but what are we to be used for? When we believe the truth "I have a purpose," we likely know why or how we are of use. What does having a purpose look like?

> **Purpose:** *noun* the reason for which something exists or is done, made, used, etc.; an intended or desired result; end; aim; goal; *verb* to set as an aim, intention, or goal for oneself[47]

One of the avenues we can take to arrive at the truth of having a purpose is to see the reason behind our existence.

---

47  *Dictionary.com*, s.v. "Purpose," accessed November 1, 2018, https://www.dictionary.com/

**What areas in your life *do* you know the reason for your involvement?**

_____

_____

_____

_____

**What areas in your life do you *not* know the reason for your involvement?**

_____

_____

_____

_____

The first question to tackle in this chapter is: Can we know for sure there is a reason for which we are made?

> *The LORD has made everything for its purpose, even the wicked for the day of trouble. Proverbs 16:4 ESV*

In the above passage we see the answer is "yes." Everything God makes, he makes with purpose. For what purpose have we been created?

> *"Do not be afraid, for I am with you; I will bring your children from the east and gather you from the west. I will say to the north, 'Give them up!' and to the south, 'Do not hold them back.' Bring my sons from afar and my daughters from the ends of the earth— everyone who is called by my name, whom I created for my glory, whom I formed and made." Isaiah 43:5-7 NIV*

As Isaiah simply states, God made us for his glory. Which brings us to the question, how do we glorify God?

**Glorify:** *verb* to give glory to (as in worship)[48]

---

48   *Merriam-Webster's Dictionary and Thesaurus,* Updated Edition, s.v. "Glorify."

For this lesson, we are going to focus on glorification in the form of worship. For most of us, when we think of what worship looks like, we will first think about worship in the form of musical worship. Now, I'm not here to discount the divine nature of musical worship, however, the concept of what worship is goes far beyond music. When we limit our worship to only musical worship, we miss out on so much of the multi-faceted goodness God offers. What other areas can we use to glorify and, in turn, worship God?

> **<u>Our words</u>:** *Because your love is better than life, my lips will glorify you. Psalm 63:3 NIV*
>
> **<u>Our body</u>:** *Or do you not know that your body is a temple of the Holy Spirit within you, whom you have from God? You are not your own, for you were bought with a price. So glorify God in your body. 1 Corinthians 6:19-20 ESV*
>
> **<u>Our actions</u>:** *"You are the light of the world. A town built on a hill cannot be hidden. Neither do people light a lamp and put it under a bowl. Instead they put it on its stand, and it gives light to everyone in the house. In the same way, let your light shine before others, that they may see your good deeds and glorify your Father in heaven." Matthew 5:14-16 NIV*

Whether we worship God, money, or some man-made idol, each of us worships something. If someone followed us around and observed our words, body, and actions, what would their answer be if we asked them what they think we worship?

Had this question been asked about me before I remade the commitment to live my life for God, others would have said worship acceptance from other people. Although I've never been one to lie to people to convince them to like me, I very much held back what I shared with people about my true character. The less people knew, the less possibility they would not accept something about me, right? I neglected the health of my body as a result of drinking excessively, and my actions involved attending parties for the sole reason of connecting with people. After all, if I hadn't consistently attended those parties, I would have eventually become irrelevant in their minds and as a result, less accepted.

The irony is, I did all of this in an effort to maintain healthy relationships, when in reality, the opposite happened. What kind of friend would accept us less the more they got to know who we were? What kind of friend would stop accepting us based on seeking better health for ourselves? Not very good ones, that's who. Not every friend that I had was of that type, but some were, and I needed to begin to make some decisions for myself to determine who those people were. If I stayed on the course of associating with people I had toxic relationships with, it would do nothing but continue to distract me from worshipping God.

In order to live a life focused on glorifying God, we must put God first. This requires us to surrender any idols we place above him. In my own life, this meant surrendering many of my friendships. It was a necessary decision for me to step into a space where I was capable of rediscovering God's love for me, but it was by no means an easy move to make. A product of that action was that I entered into a season of isolation.

I wasn't making a worship-based decision when I separated myself from these people, but I knew in my heart it was the right move. I didn't trust God, but I did trust my own ability to make the "right" decisions. Thankfully, God is extremely gracious and uses all things for the good of those who love him. I just needed to figure out how to love him.

It is true that God will ask those who follow him to surrender certain areas of their life. Luckily for us, he never does so without planning on giving us something better in return. The truth that God always gives us something better in return is by itself something to be admired and praised. What other entity that people worship can promise that?

**How do you glorify God with your words, body, or actions?**

_____

_____

_____

_____

**Which of those areas is the hardest for you to glorify God with and why?**

_____

_____

_____

_____

**How can you encourage those around you to find the beauty in showing more honor, praise, admiration, and worship to God?**

_____

_____

_____

_____

## Lesson 2: Desired Results

How often do we walk into a situation in which we truly have no desired result? I'm going guess the answer to that questions is "almost never." We live in a very purpose-driven society who feeds off of results. The majority of our actions are to some degree motivated by the anticipation of the desired result we see from them. Results are an inescapable phenomena. No action of any kind is taken without a result that occurs.

In physics, this phenomena is described in Newton's third law of motion: "For every action there is an equal and opposite reaction." Take a car accident for example: any time a car crashes into the car in front of it, the car initiating the crash gets sent backwards by an opposing force from other car. Car accidents are the result of an action that takes place, and I'm willing to bet that none of us truly desire to get in a car accident anytime soon.

In any given situation we face throughout our lives, we form an opinion of the desired outcome. If the actual outcome is anything other than our desired outcome, seeing the purpose hiding behind the situation becomes difficult.

This same logic then applies to any project or relationship we engage in. When any project, relationship, or friendship we have plays out differently from our desired outcome, we start to question the purpose of our involvement.

**Describe a situation where the actual result differed from your desired result.**

_____

_____

_____

_____

**Since the situation has passed, are you able to see how God's desires for the situation were different than yours? Does knowing that allow you to more easily see your purpose for involvement?**

_____

_____

_____

_____

Just as each of us has our own desires, God has desires for each of us. The ideal scenario occurs when each of our desires align with God's. This result however, just like every other result, cannot occur without an action taking place first. We need to first submit our opinion of what's best for our lives to God.

Why in our right mind would we want to do that, though? When we align our desires with God's, we become capable of retrieving a much more holistic view of our purpose. What does God desire for us?

> _He has saved us and called us to a holy life—not because of anything we have done but because of his own purpose and grace. This grace was given us in Christ Jesus before the beginning of time, but it has now been revealed through the appearing of our Savior, Christ Jesus, who has destroyed death and has brought life and immortality to light through the gospel. 2 Timothy 1:9-10 NIV_

God desires for us not to live driven by anything we do, but by what he already did. Above all else, he desires a relationship with us. Our capability of cultivating a relationship with God was made possible not by anything we will ever do, but by what Jesus did on the cross. When we accept the fact that it is *only* by God's grace and nothing else that we are saved, our relationship with God thrives. However, as stated previously, our desires often do not align with God's. What results occur when we live our lives according to human desires?

> *What causes fights and quarrels among you? Don't they come from your desires that battle within you? You desire but do not have, so you kill. You covet but you cannot get what you want, so you quarrel and fight. You do not have because you do not ask God. When you ask, you do not receive, because you ask with wrong motives, that you may spend what you get on your pleasures. James 4:1-3 NIV*

Living a life of human desires results in very undesirable outcomes. Sometimes, those undesirable outcomes result from our human desires being in unhealthy places. Other times, those undesirable results come when our desires are similar in nature to God's, but with the wrong motives.

In my own case, the desire to have an intimate relationship was in itself healthy. After all, God did sacrifice his one and only son for us to have that level of relationship with him. My desire was unhealthy because it came with improper motives. I was indifferent about who I had that relationship with. As for God? Not so much. He wanted me to have that relationship with *him.*

As always, God's desire was better. I never received the level of intimacy I wanted in a relationship because I only had relationships with other people on this earth. The type of intimacy I wanted in a relationship is only possible in a relationship with God, intimacy not rooted in physical touch, but in knowledge and love. I wanted to be fully known and fully loved—we all do.

Before I could get to that level of intimacy in a relationship with God, I would need to overcome some of my own internal battles. Two of those major battles were: believing God's desire to have a relationship with me as more than just head knowledge and me surrendering my expectations for what a relationship needed to look like.

Surrendering some of my unhealthy relationships and entering a season of isolation was just the beginning of this long process. Initially, the surrender created an intense pain. I placed so much of my identity in my relationships that giving them up left behind a God-sized hole in my heart. I had no intention of letting God fill that void, but I knew it couldn't stay empty either. My method of filling the void came in the form of increasing the amount I drank.

Greater amounts of pain came with a greater demand to forget the pain existed. I wanted to forget the fact that I needed to figure myself out. I had no desire to get to know myself better.

The only way I was going to get to know myself better was if I got to know God better. God knows everything about us. He simply wants us to spend time with him, get to know him, and trust he's got our back and knows what path in life best suits us. None of us will ever live all three of those aspects out perfectly, but we can all rest assured that God's grace makes up for it every time we fall short.

**What struggles do you face in aligning the desires for your life with God's?**

_____

_____

_____

_____

**How have you previously called upon God's grace to help you live out his desires for your life?**

_____

_____

_____

_____

## Lesson 3: Setting Goals

Suppose we just spent the day interviewing candidates for an open position in our company. We interviewed two candidates who had similar work and life experiences, but we're only allowed to pick one. Upon reviewing their responses, we make the observation that candidate A is particularly good at communicating how what they have achieved aligns with past goals they set for themselves. Meanwhile, candidate B places no structure in communicating how they reached their accomplishments, they just "happened." With that as our only differentiating factor, which one do we pick? The likely response is candidate A, but why?

Although goals themselves are not our ultimate purpose we aim to fulfill, they provide good illustrations for the purpose of events along the way. Goals help to define what we're working toward and our plan to get there.

This concept is seen in the definition, "to set as an aim, intention, or goal for oneself."[49] When we set goals, we bring definition to our path. This in turn helps us see the purpose in events happening along the way, including when those events don't go as desired.

The more I dug myself deeper into a relational hole, the less of a desire I had in wanting to figure myself out. I certainly wasn't going to set any goals to help with figuring myself out because ignoring the pain was too easy. Along with my lack of goals came the lack of a path to walk on. Having no path didn't really matter to me at the time, I was in too dark of a space to see a path had there been one anyway. My undefined path remained more than acceptable so long as my surroundings operated within my range of desirable outcomes. Any time my range was exceeded, I found little hope because I had no foundation of knowledge for healthy types of goals to set. My perceived "greater purpose" was, in reality, not great at all. However, God has used all of my experiences from that season for a greater purpose: bringing glory to God.

**Where in life are you currently unable to see a connection to a greater purpose? Have you set any goals to better define the greater purpose?**

_____

_____

_____

_____

---

49   *Dictionary.com*, s.v. "Purpose," accessed November 1, 2018, https://www.dictionary.com/

**What is a previous goal you set and how did it help bring purpose either to you or the situation?**

_____

_____

_____

_____

_____

God is capable of redeeming everything in our story. What types of goals should we set in order to live out the purpose God calls us to? If we take the purpose stated previously in this chapter, bringing glory to God, we should align our goals with the same types of goals set in scripture. The Bible presents us with a few areas upon which we can set goals:

Love: *The goal of this command is love, which comes from a pure heart and a good conscience and a sincere faith. 1 Timothy 1:5 NIV*

Unity: *My goal is that they may be encouraged in heart and united in love, so that they may have the full riches of complete understanding, in order that they may know the mystery of God, namely, Christ, in whom are hidden all the treasures of wisdom and knowledge. Colossians 2:2-3 NIV*

Equality: *At the present time your plenty will supply what they need, so that in turn their plenty will supply what you need. The goal is equality, as it is written: "The one who gathered much did not have too much, and the one who gathered little did not have too little." 2 Corinthians 8:14-15 NIV*

These verses lay out qualities to assist in accomplishing our purpose: a pure heart, good conscience, sincere faith, love, and the supplication of needs. When we live a life in possession of these qualities, goals centered on love, unity, and equality will begin to come to fruition in our life. As a result, we are then able to live more fully in the ways God purposed for us.

**How do you currently exemplify a pure heart, good conscience, sincere faith, love, or supplying needs in your life?**

_____

_____

_____

_____

_____

**How do you see the products of love, unity, and equality in those situations?**

_____

_____

_____

_____

_____

**What weighs you down from exemplifying a pure heart, good conscience, sincere faith, love, or supplying needs in all aspects of your life?**

_____

_____

_____

_____

## Lesson 4: Relevance

In today's society, the need to stay relevant in knowledge and experience carries more weight than ever before. Gaining knowledge has never been easier or more accessible, and this ease of access allows for the innovation of technologies to occur at an extremely rapid pace. If those innovations applied to our field of work and we failed to keep up on learning them, we would find our employer seeing us as less relevant for accomplishing the purpose they hired us for.

For the last lesson of this chapter we will look to the meaning of the phrase "to the purpose" which is, "relevant; to the point."[50] When trying to define purpose, we often look to the relevance of certain people or tasks involved. We assign a greater value to the things or people with more relevance to the task at hand. The purpose of their involvement is more apparent. What exactly gives an item relevance?

**Relevant:** *adjective* bearing upon or connected with the matter in hand; pertinent[51]

Two main components involved in relevance are: a bearing of something and our being connected to it. To stay relevant at our jobs, we must stay connected to the evolving information that pertains to a job.

If a sense of connection facilitates relevance, this also means that feelings of disconnection can lead to feelings of irrelevance. These feelings of irrelevance range from feeling like our role on a sports team is irrelevant because we're not one of the star players, to questioning our relevance in society because we feel disconnected from the people around us.

**What areas of your life do you feel *irrelevant* in and why?**

_____

_____

_____

_____

50  *Dictionary.com,* s.v. "Purpose," accessed November 1, 2018, https://www.dictionary.com/
51  *Dictionary.com,* s.v. "Relevant," accessed November 1, 2018, https://www.dictionary.com/

**What areas of your life do you feel *relevant* in and why?**

_____

_____

_____

_____

When we find our identity in the things of this world, feelings of irrelevance come easily. As we lose prior knowledge, because we don't put that knowledge to regular use, and as our bodies decay and disable us from doing tasks we used to take for granted, our relevance to those tasks and subject areas decays along with it.

In my own life, I yearned for relevance within my relationships and social standings among people. As long as I kept up my pattern of late nights with my trusted group of friends, relevance was never an issue.

This remained true until my body suddenly decided my relevance needed to be found elsewhere. Overnight, I went from being able to indulge in alcohol, consuming a six-pack by myself in a few hours, to being incapable of consuming one drink without throwing up later. In my own act of rebellion, I continued my habits anyway. The pain of losing my relevance among social circles far outweighed the effects drinking began to have on my body. I was already in the process of removing myself from certain friendships, which created enough of its own pain in my social life. There was no way was I going to let other influences tell me to remove more. Determined to prove my own body wrong, I endured the cyclical, yet temporal, pain. The pain my heart endured from this season of isolation had no end in sight, and taking any effort to distract myself from the pain, even for a night, was worth it.

Despite my interpretation of relevance, the reality is, we don't need to find our purpose or relevance in anything outside of what brings glory to God. What does relevance in the form of glorifying God look like?

> *For just as the body is one and has many members, and all the members of the body, though many, are one body, so it is with Christ. For in one Spirit we were all baptized into one body— Jews or Greeks, slaves or free—and all were made to drink of*

*one Spirit. For the body does not consist of one member but of
many. 1 Corinthians 12:12-14 ESV*

*Instead, speaking the truth in love, we will grow to become in
every respect the mature body of him who is the head, that is,
Christ. Ephesians 4:15 NIV*

These passages indicate how all of us who belong to the body of Christ
are connected. Although the body of Christ contains many members, there is
only one body. For this concept of one body of Christ to be true, every single
member in the body of Christ has to connect to one another.

That said, becoming irrelevant to the body of Christ is *impossible*. Nothing we ever do will disconnect ourselves from the body of Christ once we
place our faith in him. Just as the parts in our physical body help one another
to function, we are to use our connection to the body of Christ to help it
function as designed.

**How does a connection to the body of Christ currently influence your life?**

_____

_____

_____

**Do any of those influences help you to more easily see your purpose? If
so, how?**

_____

_____

_____

Part of our connection in the body of Christ involves the other main
component of relevance: bearing something. We are called to help bear one
another's burdens.

*Bear one another's burdens, and so fulfill the law of Christ.
Galatians 6:2 ESV*

Just as we would help a friend carry heavy and burdensome items when moving them into a new house, we as one body in Christ are to help carry one another's life burdens. To successfully carry heavy items into a new house, many body parts are involved—our eyes give direction, our arms provide stability, and our legs facilitate mobility. Each part of the body is required to most effectively carry those items. Likewise, the roles we each play in the body of Christ must all work together to be most effective.

Ultimately, the reason any of us function as one body or have the strength to help carry one another's burdens, is because Jesus bore the burden of our sins on the cross.

*He himself bore our sins in his body on the tree, that we might die to sin and live to righteousness. By his wounds you have been healed. For you were straying like sheep, but have now returned to the Shepherd and Overseer of your souls. 1 Peter 2:24-25 ESV*

Jesus finds every single one of us relevant enough to bear our sins in his death upon the cross. When we accept his punishment for our sins, we receive the Holy Spirit—the binding factor for each of us who are connected in the body of Christ. Along with connecting us all in one body, the Holy Spirit provides a direct connection in communicating with God—the same connection that allows us to cultivate a relationship with God.

When we have a relationship with God and his Spirit lives inside of us, our lives will never again become irrelevant. No longer do we have to endure pain from unhealthy lifestyles to mean something, God gives our lives purpose. It's time for each of us to die to our sin, allow Jesus to bear our punishment, and live in the unity of being connected with the body of Christ whose purpose never fades!

**How does accepting Jesus's punishment for your sins change the way you see your purpose?**

_____

_____

_____

_____

**What areas in your life do you need healing and to return to Jesus, the Shepherd of your soul?**

_____

_____

_____

_____

Dear God,

Thank you for creating me for a specific purpose. Because of my purpose, I look to live my life in a way that glorifies you. I confess that at times I place a higher priority on my human desires than your desires for my life. As a result, I do and say things not glorifying to you. Teach me how to better glorify you by my words and actions. Thank you for providing me with achievable goals to provide a framework for the purpose in which you created me. Show me how to improve on the areas of love, unity, and equality to help me fulfill my purpose. Help me to see those areas of improvement in the way you see them, and not in a way causing me to look down on myself as not being good enough. I pray against the enemy's attempts at getting me to view myself as irrelevant. The truth is, you saw my life as relevant enough to sacrifice your one and only son who bore the weight of my sins in his death on the cross. I pray that my life is used to connect with others in your body and is a light allowing those around me to see their purpose as well.

In Jesus' name,
Amen.

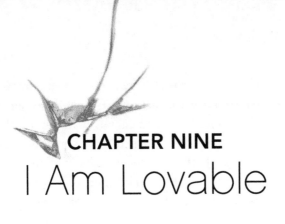

## CHAPTER NINE

# I Am Lovable

## Lesson 1: Lovable Nature

The language of love is arguably the most widely spoken and understood language in the world. It's a language that takes on countless dialects. Even if we don't feel that we possess the ability to fluently communicate love, we each desire to have love communicated to us. Every human on this earth exists with an innate craving for love. A product of our need to be loved is assessing whether or not we feel we are able to be loved.

Communicating love involves placing someone else above ourselves. In order to believe the truth "I am lovable," we must believe that we are worth that level of treatment. The message of this truth is so widely understood, that we see the message of "you are loved" communicated in one of the most widely known Bible verses:

*For God so loved the world that he gave his one and only Son, that whoever believes in him shall not perish but have eternal life. John 3:16 NIV*

What obstacles do we need to overcome in order to believe the truth "I am lovable?"

**Lovable:** *adjective* of such a nature as to attract love; deserving love; amiable; endearing[52] *adjective* easy to love: having attractive or appealing qualities[53]

---

52  *Dictionary.com*, s.v. "Lovable," accessed November 1, 2018, https://www.dictionary.com/
53  *Merriam-Webster.com*, s.v. "Lovable," accessed November 1, 2018, https://www.merriam-webster.com/

Let's first look at what it means to have a nature that attracts love. On one hand, nature is made up of the great outdoors. The natural beauty encompassed within a picturesque, mountainous landscape is hard not to fall in love with. When outdoor nature remains left untouched, it adds another dimension of lovability. National parks were born out of the concept of loving parts of nature so much, a measure of protection needed to be applied to make sure their beauty remained without the fear that they would be covered up by something else. Just as the outdoors contains nature, we as people have a nature to us as well.

**Nature:** *noun* the inherent quality or basic constitution of a person or thing[54]

The qualities of our nature are the qualities that are unable to be taken away from us. These are the same qualities given to us by God as he created us in our mother's womb. Our nature, given to us by God, is a combination of qualities no other human will ever possess. Our qualities give us character.

Living in a world where differences are often discouraged, it is easy for us to look down on our given nature. Unlike outdoor nature, we have the tendency to cover up the qualities that are inherent to our own nature. Whether our justification for covering up our nature comes from actions we took, words we said, or from a characteristic we possess, we've all felt that our particular combination of qualities is unable to be loved at some point in time. Some of us spend hours of our lives every day doing things just to get someone else to love us. Others of us struggle to believe the reality of God at times solely because we hear everyone say the cliché "God loves you," but in reality, we feel so unlovable that we tell ourselves there's no way God's love for us is true.

I continued attending parties despite the sickness I experienced because partying was a part of my nature. During that time, qualities of my nature were perceived as both lovable and unlovable by others at those parties. On the lovable side of my nature, I stayed true to who I felt I was in both my word and appearance. I was not one who would play off of a fake identity just to become the talk of a party. I regularly made appearances in clubs with jeans and no make-up on because it was never in my nature to spend hours getting ready just to win people's favor. Though no one would have ever guessed from the insecurity-driven conversations many women had as I hung out with them while getting ready for parties, the genuine nature of my appearance was highly respected and loved by most men at those same parties.

---

54  *Merriam-Webster's Dictionary and Thesaurus,* Updated Edition, s.v. "Nature."

A characteristic of my nature that wasn't as widely loved by those men was my view on romantic relationships. As many people experience when in college, I had desires of finding a relationship. I didn't know exactly how to get the relationship I wanted, but I knew having sex wasn't the answer to getting there. I partied night in and night out, failing to find the relationship I wanted. I wasn't willing to go outside of what I felt was incorrect to have sex with someone, because I was sure that things would change. I would find a relationship respectful of my desires.

**Do you possess any qualities that you feel make you *unlovable?* What are they and why do they make you feel unlovable?**

_____

_____

_____

_____

**Do you possess any qualities that you feel make *lovable?* What are they and why do they make you feel lovable?**

_____

_____

_____

_____

It makes sense that the enemy aims to attack our very nature, the qualities we cannot change about ourselves, to make us feel unlovable. Talk about an easily recurring way to cause us to feel defeated! When we find the qualities that we cannot change about ourselves as lovable, we find peace. If God is the good Creator he claims to be, what is there not to love about anything he creates? What makes believing "I am lovable" such a powerful truth? To understand the power of this truth, we must first understand what love truly is:

*Love is patient, love is kind. It does not envy, it does not boast, it is not proud. It does not dishonor others, it is not self-seeking, it is not easily angered, it keeps no record of wrongs. Love does not delight in evil but rejoices with the truth. It always protects, always trusts, always hopes, always perseveres. 1 Corinthians 13:4-7 NIV*

Love is: patient, kind, protective, trusting, and hopeful. Love is not: boastful, proud, dishonoring, or self-seeking. When we feel our nature, the make-up of our character, is lovable or able to attract love, we are indirectly telling ourselves we are worthy of others' patience, kindness, trust, and protection. In contrast, we also tell ourselves we are not worthy of attracting the products of boastful, prideful, or dishonoring behavior.

We are all able to be loved right where we are, first and foremost by God. God makes *no mistakes* in who he creates, and he keeps *no record* of our wrongs. He loves us so much, he took on the very punishment of our own wrongs upon himself. If we love God and trust in him to provide for us, he surrounds us with all of the love we ever need. All we need to do is be true to the very nature he created and intended for us.

**Given the list of characteristics of love, which do you find both the easiest and hardest to *attract* and why?**

_____

_____

_____

_____

**Which characteristic of love do you find both the easiest and hardest to *give* and why?**

_____

_____

## Lesson 2: Deserving Love

It was a late night during the middle of winter. I sat in a coffee shop, bundled up in my puffy coat and hat, and minding my own business with my freshly brewed coffee. I was about to begin some quiet time with God when a gentleman came to my table. He asked if he could draw a caricature of me, and with my permission began to sketch. He finished a rough outline of my portrait, and then paused before proceeding to draw in details of my face. "What features of yourself do you like the most?" he asked. For two reasons, I was speechless. On one hand, I don't spend a considerable amount of time obsessing over my looks—I didn't have a go-to answer. On the other, I had an immediate underlying thought of how none of my features were actually significant enough to deserve being called out over the others—how could I have a favorite?

For many of us, wrestling with the truth "I am lovable" has at some point carried those same feelings. Feelings not tied to a specific characteristic, but rather an overarching feeling of how we aren't always deserving of love. What does it look like to deserve love?

**Deserve:** *verb* to be worthy of: merit[55]

Feeling like we deserve something is a product of knowing that we are worth being loved. What does our worth look like when it comes to the topic of love? In the eyes of the world, our worthiness of love looks like doing enough of the "right" things.

For some, we grew up in a house of having to perform certain tasks for the sole reason of trying to feel more worthy of our parent's love. For others, we hide certain parts of our past where we didn't do the "right things" because we're so afraid of losing love from the world. In either case, the potential to feel unlovable prevents itself if we look to the world as our source of deserving love.

For myself, a lack of self-worth came in an emotional and a relational emptiness. While some friendships were easy to surrender initially, others came at

---

55   *Merriam-Webster's Dictionary and Thesaurus,* Updated Edition, s.v. "Deserve."

an extreme cost. I was in denial that I needed to give those friendships up for good. Because of my denial, I approached conversations with them by saying, "I really want to work things out, but right now, I need to take some time to figure myself out first. Something isn't right, I don't know what, but I'll come back when I do." I may not have valued myself enough, but I did value them. I couldn't stand being a bad influence to my friends any longer.

**Do you give yourself any qualifications for love that you don't meet? If so, what are they?**

_____

_____

_____

_____

**How often do you find yourself worthy of love? When was the last time you found yourself worthy of being loved?**

_____

_____

_____

_____

It's no secret, God loves differently than we do. How does our worthiness of love change when we look at God's love?

> For it is by grace you have been saved, through faith—and this is not from yourselves, it is the gift of God—not by works, so that no one can boast. For we are God's handiwork, created in Christ Jesus to do good works, which God prepared in advance for us to do. Ephesians 2:8-10 NIV

God's love does not require us to meet a specific list of qualifications. We will never do anything to make us more worthy of receiving God's love. God prepared our works well in advance to our arrival on this earth. Telling ourselves we are able to become more worthy of receiving God's love based off of any of our works is like telling God he is worthy of loving *himself* more because he made a good plan.

Another way we think we deserve something is if we "earned" love in some way. This type of deserving is non-existent when it comes to the topic of God's love. If we had to earn God's love, we would have to first perform an action upon which the result of our action is receiving love from God. Is that even possible?

*We love because God first loved us. 1 John 4:19*

No, it's not possible. Nothing we ever do will earn us God's love. The *only* reason we can love is because God loved us *first*. His love has always been there. He loved us before we were ever ready to receive it and his love can never be taken away from us. We cannot be separated from God's love.

> *For I am convinced that neither death nor life, neither angels nor demons, neither the present nor the future, nor any powers, neither height nor depth, nor anything else in all creation, will be able to separate us from the love of God that is in Christ Jesus our Lord. Romans 8:38-39 NIV*

Since nothing can separate us from the love of God, anything that prevents us from believing the truth "I am lovable" is *not from God!* In fact, God finds us so deserving of love, he tells us that loving one another is one of his greatest commandments.

> *One of the teachers of the law came and heard them debating. Noticing that Jesus had given them a good answer, he asked him, "Of all the commandments, which is the most important?"*
>
> *"The most important one," answered Jesus, "is this: 'Hear, O Israel: The Lord our God, the Lord is one. Love the Lord your God with all your heart and with all your soul and with all your mind and with all your strength.' The second is this: 'Love your neighbor as yourself.' There is no commandment greater than these." Mark 12:28-31 NIV*

God gives the commandment to love our neighbor as ourselves. Who qualifies as our neighbor?

**Neighbor:** *noun* one living or located near another[56]

Note how that definition does not state a specific type or kind of person. Everyone located near us at any time is a neighbor, no exceptions. Possessing worth and meeting certain qualifications do not factor into the determination of our neighbors.

**How do you love yourself?**

_____

_____

_____

_____

**How do you love your neighbor as yourself?**

_____

_____

_____

_____

God calls us to love every single person around us in the same way we love ourselves. Why? In God's mind, they deserve that love. As Christians, we are called to have a mind like Christ.

> *In your relationships with one another, have the same mindset as Christ Jesus: Who, being in very nature God, did not consider equality with God something to be used to his own advantage; rather, he made himself nothing by taking the very nature of a servant, being made in human likeness. And being found in appearance as a man, he humbled himself by becoming obedient to death—even death on a cross! Philippians 2:5-8 NIV*

---

56  *Merriam-Webster's Dictionary and Thesaurus,* Updated Edition, s.v. "Neighbor."

**What gets in the way of you fully loving your neighbor as yourself?**

_____

_____

_____

_____

**What steps can you take to renew your mind and take on the mind of Christ to allow you to more fully love your neighbor as yourself?**

_____

_____

_____

_____

## Lesson 3: Easy to Love

Suppose we've just challenged a friend of ours to a *shot put* throwing contest. In this contest, there are two identical shot puts, one weighing one pound and the other weighing twenty-five pounds. Without telling our friend what they each weigh, we hand them the twenty-five pound shot put and say whoever throws theirs farthest wins. It goes without telling, our friend is going to lose. Much less force is required to throw a shot put weighing one pound versus one weighing twenty-five pounds. We gave them a larger barrier to overcome.

We often put up these same types of barriers when it comes to feeling lovable. We create the perception in our mind and make a list of everything someone must overcome before they are able to love us. The materials in those barriers span over a range of potential topics such as: our looks, habits, and beliefs, to name a few.

When placing barriers, we bring ourselves to the conclusion that some quality in our personality is not easy to love. The road we take to arrive to the conclusion of feeling hard to love looks different for each person. For some, the road consisted of growing up in a household in which love was rarely communicated. For others, the road consisted of never receiving the level of love in the ways they desired.

Among the qualities I felt made me hard to love was my contentment in not having sex before marriage. Contrary to messages which swarm the media, I believe nothing is gained in an unmarried relationship from having sex that cannot also be found elsewhere. Because of that, I made sure to make my boundaries clear to any man wanting to make advances on me, and if those boundaries weren't okay with him, he should find someone else. I knew full well my beliefs made me different than many of the people in my same environments. In my mind, that difference made me harder to love. Satan found great joy in leveraging my thoughts of being harder to love to cause me to feel even more unlovable.

In order for us to feel that we are harder to love than someone else, there must be a differentiator we make our basis from. If the variable was being human, we'd all be on the same level—no one would be harder to love than the person next to them.

What do we tell ourselves when we reach the conclusion of being hard to love?

**Hard:** *adjective* having difficulty in doing something[57]

Typically, when we think something is difficult, it's because we don't know *how* to do it. Which raises the question: How does one love? What are we saying is "hard" for others to give to us when we say we are hard to love?

Both showing love and being loved carry extreme importance to God. Because of this, he displays many characteristics in the Bible to paint the picture of what showing love to someone looks like.

Love is:

> **Fearless:** *There is no fear in love. But perfect love drives out fear, because fear has to do with punishment. The one who fears is not made perfect in love. 1 John 4:18 NIV*
>
> **Genuine:** *Let love be genuine. Abhor what is evil; hold fast to what is good. Romans 12:9 ESV*

---

57  *Merriam-Webster's Dictionary and Thesaurus*, Updated Edition, s.v. "Hard."

**Unconditional:** *A friend loves at all times, and a brother is born for a time of adversity. Proverbs 17:17 NIV*
**Selfless:** *The greatest love you can have for your friends is to give your life for them. John 15:13*

**Which of those qualities do you find the most difficult to both give and receive, and why?**

_____

_____

_____

_____

**Do you find any of those qualities as easy to give or receive already? If so, how did it become easy? If not, how can you ask God to remove your barriers?**

_____

_____

_____

_____

Jesus performed the most selfless act ever made by dying on the cross to show God's love for us. His death alone allows for everyone on earth to never again be separated from God's love.

Jesus was a perfect display of fearless, genuine, unconditional, and selfless love. If we tried to live all of those qualities of love out on our own power, we would all find ourselves becoming burnt out very quickly. How then, do we live in display of the qualities of God's love and do so sustainably?

*Dear friends, let us love one another, for love comes from God. Everyone who loves has been born of God and knows God. Who-*

*ever does not love does not know God, because God is love. 1
John 4:7-8 NIV*

*I love you, O LORD, my strength. The LORD is my rock and
my fortress and my deliverer, my God, my rock, in whom I take
refuge, my shield, and the horn of my salvation, my stronghold.
Psalm 18:1-2 ESV*

Our love and our strength to continue loving must come from God. Love comes as a product of both knowing God and being born of his Spirit. When we possess God's Spirit, we possess the ability to love everyone on this planet just as God does. By being born of God and using his strength as our stronghold, *we* are the people who have the ability to eliminate the culture of people who feel they are hard to love! Love is a natural response to being filled with God and his love. It's not hard, it just *happens*.

**Is it hard for you to find your strength in the Lord? Why or why not?**

_____

_____

_____

_____

**Is it easier for you to love the more you get to know God? If so, what is an
example where your knowledge of God allowed you to show love to someone you wouldn't have under your own power?**

_____

_____

_____

_____

_____

## Lesson 4: Lovable Qualities

As the commonly used adage states, "there's a first time for everything." Each of us have experienced trying something for the first time. Our decision to try something new comes from a variety of factors, such as a feeling of adventure, having a friend invite us somewhere, or reading good reviews of a product. Often times, when we try something once, we don't find the activity appealing enough to try it again. Lacking appeal is one of many reasons that the phrase "there's a second time for everything" isn't also an adage. We have a high reluctance to pursue anything more than once when the activity does not have enough appeal to desire pursuing it again.

One of the aspects of being lovable is "having attractive or appealing qualities."[58] Similar in nature to our pursuit for new experiences, we pursue relationships with people who we find appealing qualities in. What makes a quality appealing?

**Appealing:** *adjective* evoking or attracting interest, desire, curiosity, sympathy, or the like; attractive[59]

When we believe our qualities possess enough appeal to attract love, we are also saying we possess qualities capable of attracting the interest, desire, or curiosity of another person.

My quest for a more intimate relationship continued as I had not yet found someone who matched well with my personality *and* respected my physical boundaries. There were some along the way who I found matched personality wise, but didn't agree with my not wanting to have sex before marriage, and there were others who respected my boundaries but didn't match in personality. When opinions differed, most of those men would respect my opinion, agree to disagree, and find someone else. As I slowly let go of all that held me down to rediscover who I was and what I wanted, these occurrences became less frequent. The truth was, I had dug myself into a hole so deep, climbing myself out of it to try to find something better took more and more energy.

My years in this search came to a halt the evening I was raped. As a result of having my boundaries violated, I dropped to an all-time low—I had never felt more unlovable in my entire life! Any energy I had left in the tank to climb myself out of darkness, removed.

---

58   *Merriam-Webster.com,* s.v. "Lovable," accessed November 1, 2018, https://www.merriam-webster.com/

59   *Dictionary.com,* s.v. "Appealing," accessed November 1, 2018, https://www.dictionary.com/

On that same night, for the first time in years, I acknowledged God's name. I was far removed from everything I knew with no place to go. I had no choice but to cry out from the depth of my soul. I worked up the strength to lift my face toward heaven, and say, "What did I do to deserve this?" I became trapped inside of my own body with no way to escape. I had all the time in the world to get sucked into a cyclone of thoughts where anger, sadness, and unworthiness constantly rotated in my mind. In an instant, I went from thinking I was unappealing because my mindset differed from someone else's, to thinking my entire body was unappealing. On the outside, every part of me looked the same. On the inside, I lost sight of my identity.

How would my negative thoughts and feelings ever go away? Not even the sun could shine light more powerful than the intensity of my darkness. I felt used, gross, and unworthy of any guy in the future who would potentially share my same desires, who also thought sex isn't the only way to experience intimacy. No man with those same desires would ever want to touch a woman who was as disgusting and as useless as I felt.

Though my desire for a relationship remained, the way I approached that desire permanently shifted. Because I felt unworthy of any man's attention, I steered away from looking for any kind of romantic relationship. All I wanted was a female friend I felt comfortable talking to about what had happened to me. I felt unsafe talking about my struggles around most men, but I needed someone who would both listen to my story and love me anyway. I had never felt the need for a female mentor before this, and now it seemed to be too late. Who would want to get to know me in my mess? Instead of drinking to socialize, I drank out of sheer desperation for something to numb my pain. I didn't know how to love myself. I didn't know if true unconditional love could exist anymore, but if it did, I desired to find that kind of love.

When searching for love, we have qualities we find desirable in other people. Just like we have qualities we find desirable, God finds certain qualities as desirable.

> *Flee the evil desires of youth and pursue righteousness, faith, love and peace, along with those who call on the Lord out of a pure heart. 2 Timothy 2:22 NIV*

Looking at the list of qualities in the verse above, how do we become people who display righteousness, faith, love, and peace?

**Righteousness:** *Therefore confess your sins to each other and pray for each other so that you may be healed. The prayer of a righteous person is powerful and effective. James 5:16 NIV*
**Faith:** *Jesus replied, "Truly I tell you, if you have faith and do not doubt, not only can you do what was done to the fig tree, but also you can say to this mountain, 'Go, throw yourself into the sea,' and it will be done. If you believe, you will receive whatever you ask for in prayer." Matthew 21:21-22 NIV*
**Love:** *"You have heard that it was said, 'Love your neighbor and hate your enemy.' But I tell you, love your enemies and pray for those who persecute you, that you may be children of your Father in heaven. He causes his sun to rise on the evil and the good, and sends rain on the righteous and the unrighteous." Matthew 5:43-45 NIV*
**Peace:** *...do not be anxious about anything, but in everything by prayer and supplication with thanksgiving let your requests be made known to God. And the peace of God, which surpasses all understanding, will guard your hearts and your minds in Christ Jesus. Philippians 4:6-7 ESV*

Each of these desirable qualities are driven by one common denominator: prayer. I veered off of the path God desired for my life until I came to a spot where I literally had no place to go mentally or emotionally. In this space of hopelessness was where I felt compelled to pray for the first time in years. My body felt disgusting and I had no way of knowing how to rid myself of those feelings on my own. I knew what happened to me wasn't my fault, but I needed answers. I had no one else to turn to, so I asked God, "Why me?"

Even though I hadn't made the effort to talk to God in years, he was still that someone I knew I could reach out to when I needed something. He was still the same guy who took away my nightmares when I made my first prayer many years prior. Deep down, I always knew God was real. He was always with me, I had just gone a really long time without dropping low enough to find him buried in my heart.

My reason for needing God at that time was certainly not something that he ever wants to see any of his children go through, but God *always* uses our circumstances for good. It was the night I was raped where I turned my head in the direction of the *right* relationship—a relationship with God.

**What makes prayer such an appealing quality to God?**

_____

_____

_____

_____

Prayer is our avenue for communication with God. God desires nothing more than for us to have a relationship with him. In fact, his desire is so strong, he allowed his son die on behalf of our sins to make that relationship possible. We all to have the ability to communicate to God by receiving the Holy Spirit that Jesus left with us as a result of his death on the cross.

> *"Nevertheless, I tell you the truth: it is to your advantage that I go away, for if I do not go away, the Helper will not come to you. But if I go, I will send him to you." John 16:7 ESV*

We do *not* serve a God who holds back on us. Jesus died and made himself nothing to give us everything. God loves each and every one of us unconditionally and eagerly awaits for each of us to pursue a relationship with him by receiving his Holy Spirit. A relationship with God is the only relationship any of us will ever enter and *receive everything*. He provides our every need, whether we know we have the need or not.

**What prevents you from fully believing you will receive whatever you ask for in prayer?**

_____

_____

_____

_____

**Have you ever experienced the peace that comes as a result of prayer? What did that peace look or feel like?**

_____

_____

_____

_____

**Do you ever experience a desire to pray? If so, what gives you that desire? If not, what about prayer is undesirable to you?**

_____

_____

_____

Dear God,

Please give me your eyes to see your love for me and the qualities you created as a part of my nature. I ask for your wisdom to help me live a life that exhibits the characteristics of love. Characteristics such as patience, kindness, trust, and hope. Thank you for being a God who loves me so much. You say no height or depth separates me from your love. I pray against anything causing my blindness to the overwhelming love you have for me, the blindness that leads me to believe I am a hard person to love. Reveal to me the ways you call me to show love to those around me through fearlessness, friendliness, and selflessness. Help me to successfully show love to others by reminding me how you are both my love and my strength. I pray these things with the faith that you are a Father who moves mountains and loves to provide for my needs. Remove any anxiety present in my life, and replace my anxiety with your peace that surpasses all understanding.

In Jesus' name,
Amen.

# CHAPTER TEN
# I Am Beautiful

## Lesson 1: Beauty Standards

In society today, we see and hear messages that are constantly trying to tell us the correct standards for beauty. Each message communicates different opinions of those standards. Some say beauty comes from making our face look a certain way, others say beauty comes from reaching a certain weight. When we compare ourselves to those messages, we often find beauty in the wrong places. Much of society agrees that beauty standards in the media are incorrect, but what are the correct standards?

Before defining the true standards for beauty, we must first understand the nature of beauty.

> **Beauty:** *noun* the quality present in a thing or person that gives intense pleasure or deep satisfaction to the mind, whether arising from sensory manifestations (as shape, color, sound, etc.), a meaningful design or pattern, or something else (as a personality in which high spiritual qualities are manifest)[60]

Some of us when thinking about beauty in the form of a pleasing quality will immediately draw our mind back to thinking about physical qualities. However, I want to challenge those thoughts and gear our minds toward discovering how more than just our looks provide pleasure.

We are all familiar with qualities we find pleasing, but what qualities, if present in us, bring intense pleasure to God? To no surprise, physical looks aren't on the list. We all receive physical beauty as a product of being God's

---

60  *Dictionary.com*, s.v. "Beauty," accessed November 1, 2018, https://www.dictionary.com/

creation. It isn't a matter of *if* we have physical beauty, physical beauty is something everyone inherits as a product of God creating them. God created each of us in his image. There is no image of God that isn't beautiful!

We do not have control over our physical nature, but we do have control over our actions. How can we make sure the actions we take please God? The Bible contains no shortage of references where God expresses pleasure. Actions associated with his pleasure are:

**Faith:** *No one can please God without faith, for whoever comes to God must have faith that God exists and rewards those who seek him. Hebrews 11:6*

**Obedience:** *To be controlled by human nature results in death; to be controlled by the Spirit results in life and peace. And so people become enemies of God when they are controlled by their human nature; for they do not obey God's law, and in fact they cannot obey it. Those who obey their human nature cannot please God. Romans 8:6-8*

**Trust:** *His pleasure is not in strong horses, nor his delight in brave soldiers; but he takes pleasure in those who honor him, in those who trust in his constant love. Psalm 147:10-11*

God didn't create us to be apart from him, our sin set us apart from him. God wants us to draw near to him by trusting in his love, placing our faith in him to know the best path for our lives, and living in obedience to doing what he says.

After the night I was raped, I entered a season where my mind was the *last place* I wanted to stay. Pleasure and delight fell to the bottom of my list of influences over my mind. The only thoughts I could play in my mind were the events of that night and how ugly I felt as a result. These constant, negative, thoughts in my head were only ever of myself. This situation left me with a barrier for communicating my feelings of ugliness to others, I didn't have those same feelings about them. I wanted to feel beautiful, I wished to feel desirable again, but the thoughts of unworthiness overpowered me.

At this time, my knowledge that God wanted to reveal the worth he saw in me still remained absent, so I pursued what I decided to be the next best thing. I decided that if I could just distract my mind enough, having no thoughts or care for myself was better than the constant negativity. The only way that I knew how to achieve that distraction was to continue my excessive drinking. I didn't want to put my faith or my trust in myself any longer, but I knew no other way. I was ready to place my obedience elsewhere, but wouldn't do so until I became convinced that obedience elsewhere was worth it.

**How can you make faith, obedience, or trust a greater part of your everyday life?**

_____

_____

_____

_____

**Can you recall a time when you demonstrated faith, obedience, or trust and felt God's pleasure?**

_____

_____

_____

_____

**Where do you feel God calling you to step out further in faith, obedience, or trust in his provision for you?**

_____

_____

_____

_____

In addition to finding beauty in pleasing qualities, beauty is found in qualities that bring satisfaction. Upon writing this lesson and searching for what brings satisfaction to God, I was led to this simple conclusion: God *is* satisfaction. The Bible addresses in many different ways that God is the source of satisfaction. This caught me off guard at first, but after seeing that synonyms of the word "satisfaction" are words like fulfillment, atonement, and joy,[61] the fact that God is the ultimate source of satisfaction became clear. He perfectly embodies all of the qualities synonymous to satisfaction. God sent his son Jesus to live on this earth as a fulfillment of the Law, to serve as an atonement for our sins through his death on the cross, and to provide us with eternal joy through the gift of the Holy Spirit. God brings satisfaction in our day to day lives through a variety of avenues:

**Guidance**: *When you pray, I will answer you. When you call to me, I will respond. "If you put an end to oppression, to every gesture of contempt, and to every evil word; if you give food to the hungry and satisfy those who are in need, then the darkness around you will turn to the brightness of noon. And I will always guide you and satisfy you with good things. I will keep you strong and well. You will be like a garden that has plenty of water, like a spring of water that never goes dry. Your people will rebuild what has long been in ruins, building again on the old foundations. You will be known as the people who rebuilt the walls, who restored the ruined houses." Isaiah 58:9-12*

**Food**: *All living things look hopefully to you, and you give them food when they need it. You give them enough and satisfy the needs of all. Psalm 145:15-16*

**Love**: *Satisfy us in the morning with your unfailing love, that we may sing for joy and be glad all our days. Psalm 90:14 NIV*

My new season of life began with a search to find the beauty I had taken away from me. I thought I was a lost cause. This search began in my place of extreme darkness. Internally, I was in ruins. I had no idea how to get to a place where on the inside, I felt like a beautiful person. In the midst of my darkness, God began to guide my steps in the way of his light.

The first of those steps consisted of removing myself from even more of the people I spent a significant amount of my time with. Someone could have easily looked at my situation from an ungodly perspective and thought "How

---

61    *Thesaurus.com,* s.v. "Satisfaction," accessed November 1, 2018, https://www.thesaurus.com/

could God be 'good' and remove so many of the very things she wanted most: relationships?" In order to rebuild on the old foundation in Christ I received during my childhood, getting rid of what currently stood on that foundation was a necessity. What stood on my foundation was a pile of unhealthy relationships that needed to be shoveled away. The pain of having fewer places to go and fewer people to talk to was real. At the same time it was oddly, yet not surprisingly, satisfying. Ultimately, the *only* relationship we ever need to find satisfaction is a relationship with God.

**When was a time when you tried to gain satisfaction from something other than God?**

_____

_____

_____

_____

**How could God satisfy those same wants or needs in your answer to the question above?**

_____

_____

_____

_____

~~~~~~~

## Lesson 2: Inner vs. Outer Beauty

When God created man and woman, he created us all to have inner and outer beauty. Both our inner and outer beauty serve as an expression of himself. The culture of our world focuses primarily on our outer beauty. We want to know how to sustain our outer beauty for as long as possible, because if we don't, we'll somehow lose value as a person. What value are we really trying to sustain in those efforts?

Looking at how beauty "gives intense pleasure or deep satisfaction,"[62] how might we look at this from a sense of ones' outer beauty?

**What characteristics in your *own* outer beauty do you find pleasing or satisfying?**

_____

_____

_____

_____

**What characteristics in *others'* outer beauty do you find pleasing or satisfying?**

_____

_____

_____

_____

Were there any differences or gaps existing within the answers to those questions? We often grade our own outer beauty on much harsher standards than we do others. We all have significantly more time to analyze our own outer appearance than we do anyone else's. Greater time for analysis gives us that much more time to declare our own imperfections. In reality, many of those attributes we find imperfect about ourselves are characteristics other people never even notice to begin with.

---

62 *Dictionary.com,* s.v. "Beauty," accessed November 1, 2018, https://www.dictionary.com/

Almost every one of us carries some degree of imbalance in the viewpoints of our own outer beauty versus the outer beauty of others. God on the other hand, views us all in the same, perfect, lens. God sees all of our outer appearances as beautiful. He sees parts of himself when he looks at us because we are all created in his image.

*So God created mankind in his own image, in the image of God he created them; male and female he created them. Genesis 1:27 NIV*

The truth is, our outer appearance is a direct reflection of God. He thought about every detail of us in advance. No part of us is a "mistake."

We are all well versed in the view we have for our self, but how does God see us?

*How beautiful you are, my love; how perfect you are! Song of Songs 4:7*

Just as Solomon saw the girl he was describing in the verse above as perfect, God sees each of us as perfect. As the commonly used phrase states, "beauty is in the eyes of the beholder," in our case, the beholder is God.

It's a fact: our outer appearance will change over time. However, does knowing this fact mean we should chase ways to sustain our outer beauty?

*So we do not lose heart. Though our outer nature is wasting away, our inner nature is being renewed day by day. 2 Corinthians 4:16 ESV*

In this passage, we see that the beauty we should seek to renew is our inner beauty. Even though our outer beauty changes over time, we can renew our inner beauty daily. When we believe the lies that Satan feeds us with regard to our "imperfect" outer beauty, all we do is allow him to distract us from focusing on our unfading beauty—our inner beauty. We do not have control over physical aging, but we do have a large degree of control over renewing our inner beauty on a daily basis.

What does renewing our inner beauty look like? In order to renew our inner beauty, we must be aware of what we're renewing.

*You should not use outward aids to make yourselves beautiful, such as the way you fix your hair, or the jewelry you put on, or the dresses you wear. Instead, your beauty should consist of your true inner self, the ageless beauty of a gentle and quiet spirit, which is of the greatest value in God's sight. 1 Peter 3:3-4*

*But the LORD said to him, "Pay no attention to how tall and handsome he is. I have rejected him, because I do not judge as people judge. They look at the outward appearance, but I look at the heart." 1 Samuel 16:7*

Qualities of our inner beauty are: living as our true and inner self, having a gentle and quiet spirit, and a good heart.

As I wandered through darkness and struggled to find my inner beauty, I lost sight of my "true and inner self." When I removed myself from social circles I was previously a part of, I began the search for a replacement. I retreated in nature to my elementary school-aged self and became shyer around people. I didn't want to be friends with all the ugliness I saw and felt inside, and I didn't expect anyone else to want to either.

At the time, I had started new classes. I noticed a girl who shared two classes with me. From a couple of weeks of seeing her interact with people before and after class, I knew that she had something I didn't. I could see joy, and I wanted to know more. I knew from the gear she lugged to class that she played soccer. Being a soccer player myself, I knew at a bare minimum we shared that passion. This common ground made for a safe talking point. The morning class we shared was in a large lecture hall and presented little opportunity to talk to classmates. However, our afternoon class took place in a small computer lab, so I made my way to the last row to sit next to her and introduce myself. Little did I know my entire life would change just from this one interaction.

The pursuit of those new environments allowed me to start searching for my true, inner beauty. The enemy will do anything he can to prevent us from discovering our inner beauty. We must not lose heart along the way, and we must continue to make the efforts to renew it daily.

**What barriers prevent you from expressing your true and inner self, having a gentle and quiet spirit, or a good heart, in a way that is pleasing to God?**

---

---

---

---

**What steps can you take to renew your inner beauty?**

_____

_____

_____

_____

## Lesson 3: Feeling Beautiful

What does it mean to stay in shape? Without even saying what type of shape, I'm guessing most of us are thinking about staying in shape physically. To stay in shape physically, physical exercise of some kind must take place on a consistent basis. We can't expect to work out for a couple of weeks and be in perfect physical shape. The type of physical shape we are in depends on how much we push ourselves in physical exercise. If all we ever do is run one mile every day, we shouldn't expect to be successful at running the marathon we signed up for come race day.

What it means to stay in shape also rings true in a spiritual context. Exercising in any context invokes a variety of different *senses*, as seen in the aspect of beauty that, "arises from sensory manifestations (as shape, color, sound, etc.)"[63] To make spaces well accommodating for physical exercise, gyms put great detail into the layout of their facilities. Is it inviting? Are the machines spaced out enough? Just as a gym invites us in to the building to use their equipment, God invites us into his story to equip us. Accepting the invitation to join God's story generates far greater value than anything gained from physical exercise.

> *Physical exercise has some value, but spiritual exercise is valuable in every way, because it promises life both for the present and for the future. This is a true saying, to be completely accepted and believed. 1 Timothy 4:8-9*

When we invite God into our lives, we become a part of his story rather than our own. Becoming a part of God's story allows us to receive the gift of true, eternal life. Participating in God's story involves the concept of spiritual exer-

---

63  *Dictionary.com,* s.v. "Beauty," accessed November 1, 2018, https://www.dictionary.com/

cise and spending consistent time with him. The passage in 1 Timothy tells us the importance of spiritual exercise. Not only does it promise us life in the present, but also for the future. What steps can we take to practice spiritual exercise?

*We struggle and work hard, because we have placed our hope in the living God, who is the Savior of all and especially of those who believe. Give them these instructions and these teachings. Do not let anyone look down on you because you are young, but be an example for the believers in your speech, your conduct, your love, faith, and purity. Until I come, give your time and effort to the public reading of the Scriptures and to preaching and teaching. Do not neglect the spiritual gift that is in you, which was given to you when the prophets spoke and the elders laid their hands on you. 1 Timothy 4:10-14*

Timothy continues to set a foundation for areas where our lives are to be an example for God, those areas being our speech, conduct, love, faith, and purity. Looking at those five areas, all of them involve direct association with other people, except for faith. Our speech and actions influence other people on a daily basis, whether we like them to or not. Whether at work, home, or school, we are all surrounded by others we have to both talk to and show a certain conduct. In the areas of love and purity, we have to make the choice as to whether we allow them to influence our lives or not. Our relationships are heavily influenced in condition to whether we show them or not.

Our faith on the other hand, is to only be rooted in Christ. We have to find that for ourselves. No one else's faith can sustain us long term. There is great importance for those of us who do have faith in God to always be sharing our faith with others. When we share our faith with others, God uses our stories to bring his light into their heart to help them find the same faith for themselves. No one will ever get to heaven if all they do is stay dependent upon other people's faith for their well-being. How can we make sure we are properly placing our faith?

*To have faith is to be sure of the things we hope for, to be certain of the things we cannot see. Hebrews 11:1*

**Which of the five areas of spiritual exercise is the hardest for you and why?**

_____

_____

_____

_____

**Which of the five areas of spiritual exercise is the easiest for you and why?**

_____

_____

_____

_____

The Bible gives us a more tangible example of what it looks like to exercise faith through the gospel of Mark:

> *They came to Jericho, and as Jesus was leaving with his disciples and a large crowd, a blind beggar named Bartimaeus son of Timaeus was sitting by the road. When he heard that it was Jesus of Nazareth, he began to shout, "Jesus! Son of David! Have mercy on me!" Many of the people scolded him and told him to be quiet. But he shouted even more loudly, "Son of David, have mercy on me!" Jesus stopped and said, "Call him." So they called the blind man. "Cheer up!" they said. "Get up, he is calling you." So he threw off his cloak, jumped up, and came to Jesus. "What do you want me to do for you?" Jesus asked him. "Teacher," the blind man answered, "I want to see again." "Go," Jesus told him, "your faith has made you well." At once he was able to see and followed Jesus on the road. Mark 10:46-52*

This passage paints a beautiful picture regarding the influence of faith. Even after the people "scolded at him to be quiet" his response was to "shout even more loudly." We see as a result of Bartimaeus's faith the amount of healing that Jesus brings when we proclaim our faith boldly.

Faith has the capability to heal us in any area we feel brought down in. From the example in Mark, it was through the man's inability to see. In my own life, I brought myself down through my struggle to acknowledge how I could be seen as beautiful by anyone.

I continued talking to the girl in my class for the next couple of weeks—sitting behind two screens in the back of a 90-minute long class made for some quality getting to know each other time. The little she got to know of me in the first couple weeks of class was enough for her to be bold in sharing her faith with me. She invited me to join her in going to a weekly college ministry she attended. I was blown away by the fact that someone could get to know me and invite me to hang out with them elsewhere. I said "yes." Besides, if I could find whatever she possessed there, I had nothing to lose. In my head, I said "yes" to finding relationships in new places. In reality, I said "yes" to finding a relationship with God.

**Have you ever felt either people or the world telling you to be quiet when you call out to Jesus in faith?**

_____

_____

_____

**Do you act anyway when people tell you to be quiet in your faith, or do you find yourself backing away?**

_____

_____

_____

**What steps can you take to spiritually exercise more?**

_____

_____

_____

Another way we exercise spiritually is through the use of our spiritual gifts. Anyone who becomes a follower of Jesus and receives the Holy Spirit possesses spiritual gifts. God intends for us to exercise those gifts so that we further his will being done on earth as it is in heaven. What are some examples of possible spiritual gifts?

*Now to each one the manifestation of the Spirit is given for the common good. To one there is given through the Spirit a message of wisdom, to another a message of knowledge by means of the same Spirit, to another faith by the same Spirit, to another gifts of healing by that one Spirit, to another miraculous powers, to another prophecy, to another distinguishing between spirits, to another speaking in different kinds of tongues, and to still another the interpretation of tongues. All these are the work of one and the same Spirit, and he distributes them to each one, just as he determines... If one part suffers, every part suffers with it; if one part is honored, every part rejoices with it. 1 Corinthians 12:7-11, 26 NIV*

Those verses provide us with a list of some of the different spiritual gifts: wisdom, knowledge, faith, healing, prophecy, speaking in tongues, and the interpretation of tongues. These spiritual gifts represent individual parts to a body. In the body of Christ, community is essential. All of us who belong to the body of Christ are to exercise our spiritual gifts, or part of the body, in conjunction with other believers for the body to work most effectively. If we do not exercise the gifts we've been given, we allow the part of the body we've been gifted with to suffer. To exercise our spiritual gifts to their intent, we need to have the faith that God knows us well enough to know which gifts best suit us.

**Do you know your spiritual gifts? How can you exercise them in a way that is pleasing to God?**

_____

_____

_____

## Lesson 4: Source of Beauty

The most expensive purchase almost every single one of us will ever make in our life is our house. With the large amounts of money we invest into houses, any time a new house is built, an extreme amount of planning first takes place. If we were to decide to build our dream house, we would make appointments first with a builder to help us determine our needs. A great amount of back and forth communication often takes place until coming to an agreement on a house layout that best fits both our functionality and personal preferences. Once the house is built, the same level of detail takes place on determining how to design the inside canvases each barren room represents. Picking out the decorations for the inside of the house includes some combination of fabrics and furniture in patterns of our choice. Upon completion of this process, we have a house we find extreme beauty in, as seen in the definition, "a meaningful pattern or design."[64]

Similar to how houses include an extreme amount of thought to design and create, God, as the Creator and designer of every human being, puts extreme thought into the process of creating us. God planned out every one of our lives well before any one of us were ever brought onto this earth. What all is included in the blueprint God lays out before creating us? What is it he is designing?

**Design:** *noun* a preliminary sketch or plan[65]

God planned a preliminary sketch for our life, and he's the only one who knows more of what the plan for our life is than we do for ourselves.

Keeping this definition in mind as we examine the different areas in which God has designed us, we see God is the designer of:

**Our thoughts:** *LORD, you have examined me and you know me. You know everything I do; from far away you understand all my thoughts. You see me, whether I am working or resting; you know all my actions. Even before I speak, you already know what I will say. You are all around me on every side; you protect me with your power. Your knowledge of me is too deep; it is beyond my understanding. Psalm 139:1-6*

---

64    *Dictionary.com,* s.v. "Beauty," accessed November 1, 2018, https://www.dictionary.com/
65    *Merriam-Webster's Dictionary and Thesaurus,* Updated Edition, s.v. "Design."

In the first part of this Psalm, we see a correlation to just how deeply God knows every one of us. He knows everything we do or think. There's nothing we can hide from him. He surrounds us on all sides. There's nothing we can do to plan our thoughts in a way he cannot hear them. He is always a part of the design and uses all things for good. As the well-known saying states, "if you can't beat them, join them." We'll never be able to beat God, he enables us with the ability to think. Instead, we should welcome his presence in joining us.

**What can you do to keep your thoughts pure, pleasing, and in turn beautiful, to God?**

_____

_____

_____

_____

**<u>Our journey</u>:** *Where could I go to escape from you? Where could I get away from your presence? If I went up to heaven, you would be there; if I lay down in the world of the dead, you would be there. If I flew away beyond the east or lived in the farthest place in the west, you would be there to lead me, you would be there to help me. I could ask the darkness to hide me or the light around me to turn into night, but even darkness is not dark for you, and the night is as bright as the day. Darkness and light are the same to you. Psalm 139:7-12*

God walks beside us with every step we take. He never leaves us, he is always there to help us wherever we go, and he shines light into any of the dark parts of our journey that we invite him into. God exposes any part of us that is not like him.

Saying "yes" to going to this college ministry and church with my new friend allowed for God to begin shining light into areas of my own life. He started by doing so in the area of alcohol. I made the decision to say "yes" to explore church again. However, I wasn't completely ready to say "no" to the bottle. For that reason, I lived a double-life of drinking on Saturday nights and waking up Sunday mornings ready to take both myself and my hangover to church.

Luckily, this church was full of people like my friend who embraced the "come as you are" characteristic of God. I was welcomed with hugs and open arms every single Sunday as I stepped up to the door. God's light began to take greater effect in my life. I knew I didn't have to put on my alcohol mask to be there, but I wasn't quite ready to discover my true self either. Regardless, going to church was a step in the right direction. The more we allow God to shine light on our path, the more capable we are of seeing the beautiful design God has for our journey.

**Where are the areas of your life in which God's light does not shine brightly?**

_____

_____

_____

_____

**What holds you back from allowing God to shine light into those areas?**

_____

_____

_____

_____

**Our appearance:** *You created every part of me; you put me together in my mother's womb. I praise you because you are to be feared; all you do is strange and wonderful. I know it with all my heart. When my bones were being formed, carefully put together in my mother's womb, when I was growing there in secret, you knew that I was there—you saw me before I was born. The days allotted* *to me had all been recorded in your book, before any of them ever began. O God, how difficult I find your thoughts; how many of them there are! If I counted them, they would be more than the grains of sand. When I awake, I am still with you. Psalm 139:13-18*

Each of us was *carefully* put together by God.

**Careful:** *adjective* cautious in one's actions; taking pains in one's work; exact; thorough; (of things) done or performed with accuracy or caution[66]

What does this mean for us? It means that God did *not* make any mistakes when creating us. When God created us, he did so cautiously, painstakingly, and performed the creation of us with the utmost accuracy. The more we understand the detail and care behind God's design for us, the more we will see the same beauty in ourselves that he sees in us.

**Are there any qualities you view as being mistakes in the way God created you?**

_____

_____

_____

God sees all of those qualities answered above in us. He saw them even before we were born, he made those qualities in us for a purpose, and he thinks they are *good*.

**What qualities about yourself do you see as being good and why?**

_____

_____

_____

_____

---

66  *Dictionary.com,* s.v. "Careful," accessed November 1, 2018, https://www.dictionary.com/

**What qualities about yourself do you see as *not* being good and why?**

_____

_____

_____

_____

〰〰〰

## Lesson 5: God's Beauty

When it comes to physical beauty, we each have preferences to certain features we find appealing. Although physical beauty isn't the most important quality in determining a life partner, physical beauty is likely a contributing factor in our attraction to another person. If someone we came across manifested every physical quality on our list of desires, our physical attraction to them would be inescapable. Similar in nature to our manifestation of physical qualities, we can also manifest spiritual qualities.

Seen in the last definition of beauty for this chapter is "a personality in which high spiritual qualities are manifest."[67] Exhibiting spiritual qualities is much less black and white as exhibiting physical qualities. Emulating spiritual qualities is a choice we all make, and doing so is against our human nature. We, as sinful humans, naturally exhibit selfish qualities. The only one who truly exhibits high spiritual qualities in their nature is God.

The good news is, God sent his son Jesus down to earth to die on the cross as a punishment for our sinful nature, so that we might believe and accept his punishment as our own. Jesus, being sinless in his own actions while here on earth, conquered death on the cross and rose to life again. When we choose to make the decision to accept Jesus's punishment for our sin, we receive the power of God's Holy Spirit. Through the gift of the Holy Spirit, we possess the ability and strength to embody the spiritual qualities that the Spirit manifests. What are those spiritual qualities?

*What I say is this: let the Spirit direct your lives, and you will not satisfy the desires of the human nature. For what our human*

---

67  *Dictionary.com,* s.v. "Beauty," accessed November 1, 2018, https://www.dictionary.com/

*nature wants is opposed to what the Spirit wants, and what the Spirit wants is opposed to what our human nature wants. These two are enemies, and this means that you cannot do what you want to do. If the Spirit leads you, then you are not subject to the Law. What human nature does is quite plain. It shows itself in immoral, filthy, and indecent actions; in worship of idols and witchcraft. People become enemies and they fight; they become jealous, angry, and ambitious. They separate into parties and groups; they are envious, get drunk, have orgies, and do other things like these. I warn you now as I have before: those who do these things will not possess the Kingdom of God. But the Spirit produces love, joy, peace, patience, kindness, goodness, faithfulness, humility and self-control. There is no law against such things as these. And those who belong to Christ Jesus have put to death their human nature with all its passions and desires. The Spirit has given us life; he must also control our lives. Galatians 5:16-25*

**How can the Holy Spirit enable you to exemplify love, joy, peace, patience, kindness, goodness, faithfulness, humility or self-control? How do these qualities differ from the qualities of your human nature?**

_____

_____

_____

_____

Beauty in this context is an outflow of allowing the Holy Spirit to shift and re-define our desires. The power of the Holy Spirit puts to rest any of the desires of the flesh. My desire to drink was slowly put to rest the more I continued to attend church. Putting my desire for drinking to rest allowed me to make decisions that influenced my desire for a relationship. I made it to a point where I figured myself out enough to go back to my old friends as promised months prior to say, "I no longer drink in the same way I used to." As expected, most of them couldn't believe I made that decision. Some friendships even ended because they weren't going to stop going to parties themselves.

I can't say that having those conversations felt good, but the peace I gained from finally pursuing actions geared toward my own beauty and not someone's perception of my beauty was freeing. The passage in Galatians states that when we allow the Spirit to direct our lives, we will not satisfy the desires of our human nature. For the first time in my life, I saw that happening. The Spirit directed me toward seeking a relationship with God and used the friends I made in church to reveal a glimpse of the beauty that a relationship with God provides.

**Which fruits of the Spirit do you find most challenging to identify with and why?**

_____

_____

_____

_____

**Have you felt the Spirit trying to direct you somewhere? If so, where to and how will you get there? If not, what is preventing that from happening?**

_____

_____

_____

_____

Dear God,

Thank you for not defining my beauty by the same standards I see in society on an everyday basis. True beauty is found in qualities that please you. Qualities such as faith, obedience, and trust. Help me to possess and refine these qualities in myself so I can live a life more pleasing and satisfying to you, because you do not look at beauty from my outer self, but from my heart. I ask for the strength to more fully exercise my faith with the spiritual gifts you have uniquely given to me and I long for your beauty to stem from all of my thoughts and journeys. May your Holy Spirit be the director for all the beauty you have planned out for my life.

In Jesus' name,
Amen.

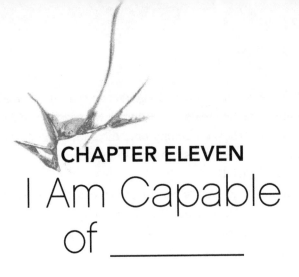

**CHAPTER ELEVEN**

# I Am Capable
# of _____

## Lesson 1: Power

It's a well-known fact, life is hard. For the most part, if we know we will make it through our situation of difficulty, we are okay with life being hard. When we see others going through hard times, we often try to remind them that things won't always be this way. We give them encouragement by reminding them of good attributes about themselves with the hope that it will help them overcome their struggle. It's easy for us to have feelings of defeat during difficult seasons. To help counteract our feelings of defeat, this verse is often quoted:

*I can do all this through him who gives me strength. Philippians 4:13 NIV*

When going through difficulty, the phrase "I am capable of _____" may seem like a lie. Whether our feelings come as a result of an argument with a good friend we thought would never be resolved, receiving the news that one of our friends or family members just passed away, or seeing a diagnosis we hoped to never face, all of us have encountered a place where we felt incapable of seeing the way out. In these times, we begin to have thoughts such as "How am I ever going to make it through this?"

We make it through those times by the strength of God.

It is critical that we never stop reading the verse Philippians 4:13 half-way at *"I can do all this…" NIV* The *key* to being able to do all things is *through*

*God's strength.* We were never meant to go through struggles on our own. God even said so himself as he created Eve that *"...It is not good for the man to be alone..."* Genesis 2:18 NIV Holding onto the knowledge that all things are capable through God's strength is of utmost importance for us to feel capable of making it through a trial.

When we tell ourselves we are capable, what exactly are we saying?

**Capable:** *adjective* having ability, capacity, or power to do something: able, competent;[68] *adjective* having power and ability; efficient; competent[69]

**Describe a situation where you felt fully capable?**

_____

_____

_____

_____

**What caused you to feel capable?**

_____

_____

_____

_____

As previously stated, feelings of capability can be hard to come by in difficult times when we don't have the strength necessary for getting through the difficulty on our own. These situations bring upon feelings of powerlessness. Feeling powerless puts us in a very defeated mood when we don't have access to a charger—the charger we're all searching for is God.

---

68  *Merriam-Webster's Dictionary and Thesaurus,* Updated Edition, s.v. "Capable."
69  *Dictionary.com,* s.v. "Capable," accessed November 1, 2018, https://www.dictionary.com/

*You see, at just the right time, when we were still powerless,*
*Christ died for the ungodly. Very rarely will anyone die for a*
*righteous person, though for a good person someone might*
*possibly dare to die. But God demonstrates his own love for us*
*in this: While we were still sinners, Christ died for us. Romans*
*5:6-8 NIV*

It is no surprise why so many of us experience feelings of powerlessness. Part of the reason we often feel powerless, and therefore incapable, is simply because in our sinful human nature, we *are* powerless. With our actions alone, we are incapable of being in the presence of God. God cannot exist in the same space as sin, for he is perfect and without sin. Therefore, God sent Jesus to earth to take on the punishment of our sins. Through Jesus's death and the gift of the Holy Spirit, we are no longer powerless, but rather *filled* with power!

*For the Spirit that God has given us does not make us timid;*
*instead, his Spirit fills us with power, love, and self-control. 2*
*Timothy 1:7*

As I began my journey to rediscover myself, I faced substantial feelings of incapability and being timid with the formation meaningful relationships with these Christian people I now spent time with. I loved both the time I spent with them and the formation of new friendships, but inside, I still felt unworthy and believed that my body was unclean.

Continuing to allow God to shine light in the area relationships, I began going to church on a consistent basis. After about a year of going back to church, I heard a message on the value our bodies have to God.

*Or do you not know that your body is a temple of the Holy Spirit*
*within you, whom you have from God? You are not your own,*
*for you were bought with a price. So glorify God in your body. 1*
*Corinthians 6:19-20 ESV*

My body? A temple? I immediately broke into tears. There was *no way* God valued my body so much! My mind still very much believed that my body was tainted, that no man could possibly appreciate it.

That message pointed a light at a very dark place in my heart. I didn't know how to feel that my body carried significant value. Although that message didn't all of a sudden cause me to feel valuable, I began a search to understand the truth behind it. If God really valued me that much, I wanted to both get to know him and figure out how that was possible.

A clear difference existed between the confidence the pastor portrayed in his message and the lack there of I felt inside. This noticeable difference was the cause of what Satan used in order to lie to me and say, "You won't ever be able to achieve the relationship and find the intimacy you want." In reality, the difference came from a difference of power. I felt the full effect of trying to "do all this," as Philippians states, on my own strength and coming up powerless instead of living out the power of the Holy Spirit inside of me.

When we die to our sinful nature and live by means of the Spirit, the formerly incapable becomes capable and any feelings that we are powerless disappear.

**What causes you to feel the effect of being powerless?**

_____

_____

_____

_____

**How can you invite the power of the Holy Spirit to help you in that area?**

_____

_____

_____

_____

## Lesson 2: Efficiency

Throughout all of elementary school, my claim to fame was established through my performance on timed tests. Timed-tests were sheets of paper which had 100 basic math problems on them. The teacher would pass them around to the whole class, face down, and not allow us to turn them right side up until at their desk with the timer in hand. With nothing but that paper and a pencil in hand, once the timer began it was a race to complete as many of the problems accurately in the given time as possible. Because of my ability to efficiently perform those calculations in my head so quickly, I always finished in first place. When it came to timed-tests, I felt extremely capable. No one could take those feelings away from me. Yet, at the same time, my dominant performance could have very well caused others in my class to feel incapable.

As for my ability to read? Not so dominant. Throughout my entire life, I've always taken longer to read and understand books than most people. For many years, I felt incapable at reading, simply by judging how long it took me to read the same content as someone else. In both instances, neither I nor my classmates were actually as incapable as we judged ourselves to be. Every single one of us was capable of completing 2 + 5 and reading a chapter book, we just used different techniques.

The next aspect of what it means to be "capable" is simply the word "efficient."[70] With a society who spends so much time in comparison mode, we can so easily fall into a trap of seeing ourselves as "incapable." This is especially true if we see someone else doing the same thing so much "better" or "faster" than us. In actuality, efficiency is much more than being the "fastest" or the "best" at anything.

**In what ways have you viewed yourself as being incapable because you know you weren't the "best" or the "fastest" at it?**

_____

_____

_____

_____

_____

70  *Dictionary.com,* s.v. "Capable," accessed November 1, 2018, https://www.dictionary. com/

The way God views efficiency and the way the world views efficiency are very different. Upon searching for scripture references speaking into the concept of efficiency, I found a recurrence to the word: diligence.

**Diligent:** *adjective* characterized by steady, earnest, and energetic effort[71]

To God, efficiency is not about how fast we get something done, or how gifted we are at getting something done. Efficiency is simply a matter of whether we make the effort to complete the work God calls us to. There is *no* comparison involved. Each and every one of us has a unique story to God. We all have a calling on our lives and we are the most efficient person to complete our calling. How is diligence described in the Bible?

*The plans of the diligent lead to profit as surely as haste leads to poverty. Proverbs 21:5 NIV*

*A sluggard's appetite is never filled, but the desires of the diligent are fully satisfied. Proverbs 13:4 NIV*

When we are diligent in living out God's calling for our life, satisfaction and profit result. What does that satisfaction and profit look like? Our profit and satisfaction often present themselves in ways we don't anticipate.

After noticing the difference in how all of the other Christian people I hung around lived with power through the Holy Spirit, I became diligent in figuring out how to experience that power for myself. God wants to have a relationship with every one of us so badly, his son Jesus died for us and left us all with the Holy Spirit, so we could directly communicate to God and form a relationship with him.

Around this time, the same friend who invited me back to church took the next step of boldness and asked to meet with me on a weekly basis. In the words of the Bible, she made me her disciple. In my words, she became the female in which I could safely talk to that I was in such desperate need of. For the remainder of the school year, we met every week at a coffee shop located in the heart of campus. Each week, we dug into a different aspect of what living a life guided by the Holy Spirit—rather than self-guidance—looks like. The one-on-one time created a safe environment for me to open up the hurt, ugliness, and unworthiness I hid. I found a person who I could trust in sharing my darkness with and, at the same time, hear both her story and how God wanted a personal relationship with me too. Meeting with her planted seeds to grow the relationship I searched for my entire life—a relationship with God.

---

71  *Merriam-Webster's Dictionary and Thesaurus,* Updated Edition, s.v. "Diligent."

Even though I didn't come to this realization in my life "faster" than she did, I was just as *capable* at having a relationship with God as she was, and she showed me how. God doesn't care how we get to the place in our life where we realize a relationship with him is what we've needed our whole life, he just cares that we *get there*. Over time, our diligence in cultivating a relationship with God leads to nothing short of complete satisfaction and profitability.

**What holds you back from diligently doing what God calls you to?**

_____

_____

_____

_____

**Can you think of an example of a time in your past where your diligence in following God resulted in being fully satisfied or provided for?**

_____

_____

_____

_____

## Lesson 3: Competency

Our brain surgeon friend just invited us as their "plus one" to join them in attending a get together with all of the region's best brain surgeons. Upon arriving to the event, we join a number of different conversations involving the latest techniques in brain surgery. Unless we perform brain surgery ourselves, there's a high likelihood much of the conversation goes straight over our heads. In environments like this, we have a tendency to see other people's level of competency as better than ours. So often we use the words "capable" and "competent" interchangeably. When we look down on our own competence in examples like these, we likely also look down on our capabilities. Unless we're a brain surgeon too, we aren't as competent or capable at performing the same procedures as they are. Can we use examples like this to view our overall capability as a person? Where does our competence come from?

**Competent:** *adjective* having suitable or sufficient skill, knowledge, experience, etc., for some purpose; properly qualified[72]

From the above definition, this lesson will focus on two themes: having sufficient skills and proper qualifications.

Feelings of insufficiency can cause us to fail to see the value we bring. The truth is, we all possess skills in different areas. However, when we are in certain situations like being surrounded by a group of brain surgeons speaking on the topic of surgery, feelings of insufficiency have a tendency to rise. It feels like we got left out somehow because others have a skill that we don't.

The problem is, this mindset does not look at the whole definition of the word "competency." We often become focused on having sufficient skills and we ignore the second half of the definition: "for some purpose." To see our true capability, not only must we own our skills, but we must also know our purpose.

God creates all of us with a purpose to fulfill. To live in full sufficiency, we must use our skills in the purpose with which we were created. If we're not using those skills, there is the potential to devalue both ourselves and our skills, as seen in the following passage:

*"You are like light for the whole world. A city built on a hill cannot be hid. No one lights a lamp and puts it under a bowl; instead it is put on the lampstand, where it gives light for everyone in the house. In the same way your light must shine before people, so that they will see the good things you do and praise your Father in heaven." Matthew 5:14-16*

We do not find competency within a community that identifies with the lamp in these verses. We hold worth, we are unique, and we cannot allow people to trample on our significance. Finding what it is that makes us shine, and then hiding our light from others due to fear of other people's opinions, is *exactly* what Satan wants us to do!

---

72  *Dictionary.com*, s.v. "Competent," accessed November 1, 2018, https://www.dictionary.com/

How do you identify with the light from the verses in Matthew with regard to hiding the unique light you've been given to shine before others? What was the result of that situation?

_____

_____

_____

_____

Name a situation where you felt sufficiently skilled. What was the result of that situation?

_____

_____

_____

_____

The verses in Matthew indicate how no one would ever put an actual lamp underneath a bowl to hide its light. If that's true, why are we so prone to overlook our own light and discount our skills?

_____

_____

_____

_____

I believe part of the answer to the last question lies within the second definition for "competency." We don't feel properly qualified. The question is: in what source do we find our qualifications?

Prior to learning what a relationship with God looked like, I turned to myself as the source of my qualifications. My true purpose in life was nowhere to be found, but I stood on the belief that as long as I tried hard enough, I could earn the qualifications I needed to get me where I wanted to go. To no surprise, I was wrong. Nothing I ever did helped me to become more qualified to fulfill my purpose.

When we only look at competency from an earthly standpoint, none of us will ever become properly qualified for fulfilling our God-given purpose. The good news is, to fulfill our God-given purpose, we need to go no further than placing our faith in him to provide us with everything we need.

*And with all his abundant wealth through Christ Jesus, my God will supply all your needs. Philippians 4:19*

When we have the faith to believe the above verse, we can live with the authority, competence, sufficiency, and qualifications necessary to fulfill our purpose.

In conjunction to meeting individually with my friend and learning more about what a relationship with God looks like, God supplied me with one of my needs—the need for a healthy community. During this time, I began attending a weekly Bible study for the first time. Attending this small group allowed me to have a safe space. In that space, I opened up about the truth behind my struggles in my relationships, my inner beauty, and everything in between. This was made possible because I knew that I could do so without feeling condemned for my struggles.

In my new community, I didn't have to pretend to be anyone but myself. The whole premise of our weekly meeting and doing life together was that we were all trying to figure out how to be the best versions of ourselves *together*.

We cultivate a great amount of power when getting involved with a group of people who realize the success of the group is more important than their individual success. No two people have the same combination of needs, and the supplication of those needs looks different for everyone. We need to be people who both place confidence in Christ to supply all of our needs and cheer on the journeys of our friends along the way as their needs are also supplied by Christ.

*Such confidence we have through Christ before God. Not that we are competent in ourselves to claim anything for ourselves, but our competence comes from God. He has made us competent as ministers of a new covenant—not of the letter but of the Spirit; for the letter kills, but the Spirit gives life. 2 Corinthians 3:4-6 NIV*

When we live life solely as an attempt to fulfill the Law, or letter as in the verse above, to find our purpose in life we will fall short every single time. We aren't capable of fulfilling the Law on our own, and if we were, we wouldn't need Jesus. When we die to ourselves and accept Jesus as our savior, we receive the Spirit which brings life. When we choose to live a life filled with the Spirit, we become capable of fulfilling every aspect of our purpose. God supplies us with every need we will ever encounter to live out our purpose.

**In what ways can you ask God to supply your needs?**

_____

_____

_____

_____

**Do you ever feel improperly qualified? How can you invite the Spirit to provide you with the competency and wealth necessary to bring life into that situation?**

_____

_____

_____

_____

## Lesson 4: Capacity

When thinking about the word "capacity," my analytically-wired brain gears toward the quantity or amount that an item is capable of holding or taking in. Say we go to the grocery store to buy milk and we make the decision to buy only a half-gallon of milk instead of a whole gallon. When we make the decision to buy only a half-gallon, we are committing to only drinking a half-gallon of milk by its expiration date.

A half-gallon carton of milk holds the capacity to store anything up to a half-gallon of milk. For any amount exceeding a half-gallon, the carton would be *incapable* of taking or holding more milk. Just as the carton limits how much milk can be held, we often implement the same concept by limiting how much we allow God to fill us. I often hear this metaphor in the context of how we "Put God in a box." Meaning, we like to build up walls to limit the amount we allow God to work within us. When we do this, we assign a specific capacity to God and limit his capacity.

**Do you ever find yourself limiting the ways you allow God to fill you up? How?**

_____

_____

_____

_____

Even though we often place limits, the truth is, God has *no limit* on how much he is willing to give us. Any capacity assigned to God is self-induced. Many factors go into building up the barriers defining our capacities: we could be comfortable with our life as is, afraid of allowing God to influence certain areas of our life, or have areas of hurt in our past which cause us to be reluctant in opening up certain parts of our life again. With regard to relationships with other people, these behaviors are, at times, healthy. However, when it comes to God, we should stop at nothing to surrender every part of our lives to him because he stops at nothing to provide us with our every need.

*If any of you lacks wisdom, you should ask God, who gives gen-
erously to all without finding fault, and it will be given to you.
James 1:5 NIV*

God gives freely and graciously to all. We are capable of doing all things
when we invite God into the process. God gives generously, and we don't have
to do anything beforehand to earn his giving.

**What has God been trying to give you?**

_____

_____

_____

_____

On the other side of the giving coin is receiving. For all things God gives
to us, we must be willing to receive them. Whenever God gives us something,
we need to be conscious of investing what he gives in the right places. When
we invest God's giving in the right places, we find a multiplication of our gifts,
as described in the following passage:

*"At that time the Kingdom of heaven will be like this. Once
there was a man who was about to leave home on a trip; he
called his servants and put them in charge of his property. He
gave to each one according to his ability: to one he gave five
thousand gold coins, to another he gave two thousand, and to
another he gave one thousand. Then he left on his trip. The
servant who had received five thousand coins went at once and
invested his money and earned another five thousand. In the
same way the servant who had received two thousand coins
earned another two thousand. But the servant who had received
one thousand coins went off, dug a hole in the ground, and
hid his master's money. After a long time the master of those
servants came back and settled accounts with them. The servant who had received five thousand coins came in and handed
over the other five thousand. 'You gave me five thousand coins,*

*sir,' he said. 'Look! Here are another five thousand that I have earned.' 'Well done, you good and faithful servant!' said his master. 'You have been faithful in managing small amounts, so I will put you in charge of large amounts. Come on in and share my happiness!' Then the servant who had been given two thousand coins came in and said, 'You gave me two thousand coins, sir. Look! Here are another two thousand that I have earned.' 'Well done, you good and faithful servant!' said his master. 'You have been faithful in managing small amounts, so I will put you in charge of large amounts. Come on in and share my happiness!' Then the servant who had received one thousand coins came in and said, 'Sir, I know you are a hard man; you reap harvests where you did not plant, and you gather crops where you did not scatter seed. I was afraid, so I went off and hid your money in the ground. Look! Here is what belongs to you.' 'You bad and lazy servant!' his master said. 'You knew, did you, that I reap harvests where I did not plant, and gather crops where I did not scatter seed? Well, then, you should have deposited my money in the bank, and I would have received it all back with interest when I returned. Now, take the money away from him and give it to the one who has ten thousand coins. For to every person who has something, even more will be given, and he will have more than enough; but the person who has nothing, even the little that he has will be taken away from him." Matthew 25:14-29*

This parable of the three servants shows us a great example of three people with very different capacities for both giving and receiving in their life. One of the servants received five thousand coins, the second received two thousand coins, and the third received one thousand coins. We also see their actions to what they were given and the results of their actions. The servant who was given the largest amount lived faithfully to what he was given and produced an additional five thousand coins. In contrast, the servant who was given only one thousand coins lived in fear and produced nothing. This parable mirrors our human nature of building up walls of fear and creating a *capacity* for which God is able to give.

When I reached a point where I attended the Bible study weekly and got involved in my church community, but I found myself treating the community

I was given exactly like the servant who had received the one thousand coins. After finding what I had been looking for all those years, there was no way I wanted to give the community up or invest it for a potentially better outcome. Out of the fear of losing the community that God provided me and the relationships that came with that community, I "dug a hole in the ground" and protected it. I was afraid of having my community taken away. At the same time, I prevented God from multiplying the gift.

I treated my community in this way because, although God did not find any faults in me, I found them in myself. My faults did not add up to thinking I deserved more than what I had already been given. As a result of both my fear and not allowing God to have full influence over that part of my life, I created a specific capacity upon which I allowed God to work within me.

It turns out, God was not completely satisfied with my behavior on this front. After a year of thriving in these growing relationships, he told me to dig up what I had been hiding, move significantly far away from my community, and find the value of what trusting God to provide looks like.

I moved across the country from everything I ever knew, leaving me with no one else's faith to fall back on but my own. The move left me with no choice but to take on the stance of the servants who received the two thousand and five thousand coins. If I dug a hole this time, I had no close personal relationships in my immediate surroundings to protect. My choices were either invest in the future potential of my new environment with the faith that new relationships would form, or dig and bury the nothing I had.

In order to invest in my relationship with God, I had to once again fully surrender the area of my relationships to him. The work of this investment required me to first build a stronger relationship with God, and second, trust he would place the new, and right, people in my life. To no surprise, God provided a similar community of women that I previously had and even gave me the space to lead a separate community of women in order to give back all that had been given to me in the years prior. I still had much to discover in the areas of the depth of both God's love for me and my calling at this point, but I knew I couldn't go wrong by trusting him. I was overjoyed to receive the opportunity to begin acting in the same capacity to other women as my friend from my class was to me a couple years prior. The fact is, if something that happens to us causes us to truly change, especially if that "something" is from God, it is impossible not to want to give back and do the same for others.

We will always be satisfied anytime we expand the capacity upon which we allow God to influence our life. He never takes anything from us without giving back more than what we started with, he never finds any faults in us, and he always gives us everything we need to succeed.

**Describe a time in your life where you were like the servant who received the five thousand coins.**

_____

_____

_____

_____

**Describe a time in your life where you were like the servant who received the one thousand coins.**

_____

_____

_____

_____

**Were there any differences in either the outcome or your feelings of those situations? If so, what?**

_____

_____

_____

_____

## Lesson 5: Influence

The world we live in constantly surrounds us with both good and bad influences. Some influences we seek out on our own accord, others we don't. We can't escape the influence that the environments surrounding us have. What role do influences play when we talk about the subject of capability?

One thing we know to be true about people or things containing influence on or over us is: we are not the same people we were before the influence entered our life. Whether we allow good influences or bad influences to affect us is largely up to us and our own free will. In either case, when we allow influences to take effect in our lives, they cause us to stand out in the way that we conduct ourselves. Influences change the way that we respond to the challenges life presents, they affect our overall demeanor, and they change our identity.

**What are some influences that have played a role in your life?**

_____

_____

_____

_____

**What role have they played in guiding you to the path you are on today?**

_____

_____

_____

_____

_____

For this last lesson we will look at what it means to be "capable of" something, which is, "open to the influence or effect of; susceptible of."[73] I specifically like that it indicates that in order to be capable of something we have to be *open* to it. This means that we need to be *willing to receive* an influencer before we allow it to affect us. Living a life of receiving and being influenced by Christ is no different.

> *Anyone who is joined to Christ is a new being; the old is gone,*
> *the new has come. 2 Corinthians 5:17*

When we invite Jesus into our lives and accept him as our savior, our lives become permanently influenced, we change, and we stand out. After making my first prayer to receive Christ in middle school, the capacity by which I allowed God to influence my life remained small for many years. Although I didn't fully embrace his influence for all those years, that night when he took away my nightmares was the beginning of becoming a changed person.

> *Now it is God who makes both us and you stand firm in Christ.*
> *He anointed us, set his seal of ownership on us, and put his*
> *Spirit in our hearts as a deposit, guaranteeing what is to come.*
> *2 Corinthians 1:21-22 NIV*

When I made the decision to rededicate my life to God during college, I did so in the search of a new community. I knew the pain that came from both not having a community and looking for community centered in things other than Christ. I never wanted either of those types of communities to be my reality again. Once I received a God-centered community, God placed a deposit in my heart to make that sure I do anything and everything it takes to be a resource for that same type of community for as many women as possible who are going through the same pain that I experienced.

The old me saw little reason for the need to hang out with groups of women. The new me, strongly influenced by God, saw too many hurting women in the world who need the hope God brings. We find hope by becoming a new creation in him—not by anything we do.

It was only a matter of weeks after I moved out west when God provided a friendship with another woman who shared my passion of bringing a Christ-centered community among women. By myself, starting a women's ministry wouldn't have been possible. I knew no one, and I had no influence in the Christian community where I lived. However, God had the influence, and

---

73   *Dictionary.com*, s.v. "Capable," accessed November 1, 2018, https://www.dictionary.com/

my new friend had the established community. Less than a couple of months later, we started up a women's ministry that focused on a different attribute of being a Godly woman each month.

On my own, I would have been incapable of having such success with starting a women's ministry. With God's involvement, we are capable of executing everything. God will *never* place a desire in our hearts without providing us with a way to be capable of fulfilling that desire. When we involve God's influence, everything succeeds. His influence transforms our capability and we become greater than we could have ever dreamed or imagined for ourselves.

On my own, I was just a person trying to find meaning in my relationships and navigating my purpose in this world. With God, my purpose was predestined. I found a relationship with him deeper than any human relationship can ever provide. I am capable of being a mentor for other women because God both placed a deposit within me and guaranteed the path my life is headed on.

**How does knowing that God has anointed you make you feel?**

_____

_____

_____

_____

**Do you feel more capable of doing what you're called to knowing God placed a deposit within you and guarantees what is to come?**

_____

_____

_____

_____

**What stops you from letting God influence all parts of your life?**

_____

_____

_____

_____

Dear God,

I pray and ask for you to supply me with the power of your Holy Spirit—a power through which I am capable of doing anything. Thank you for providing me with the fuel to act as power for completing every good work you planned for my life in advance. You are a God who honors diligence and I don't have to feel like I need to be the "best" or "greatest" at something to be capable of fulfilling your calling for my life. I ask for you to remove anything that causes me to fix my eyes on anything other than you. Give me your eyes to see for myself the unique purpose you made me for, and not as someone who operates out of incompetence. Break down the walls that hinder me from being completely filled by you, and supply me with your wisdom. I want to become a person who is capable of positively influencing others and guiding them toward your goodness. Thank you for your source of never-ending blessings and strength for me to turn to at all times as I learn and grow into the positive influence you created me to be.

In Jesus' name,
Amen.

## CHAPTER TWELVE

# I Am Not a Failure

## Lesson 1: Success

We are cultured to look at failure in a specific way from a very early age. In grade school, if we receive a failing grade, we know we received that grade because our performance in the class was not at a satisfactory level. Our failing grade means we were at the bottom of the totem pole, and we didn't do enough things correctly to grant access to the next level. If we don't eventually learn the material from the course within a certain time frame, we are held back. Getting held back often causes us to create a negative perception of ourselves. Although this is just one type of failing, the negative perception we create as a result of failing generates a culture with the fear for failure.

This fear of failure carries with us into adulthood. For some, the fear looks like thinking we fail in our relationships by not doing enough. For others, the fear looks like failing our future self because we aren't at the place in life that we expected to be at by this point. These types of thoughts are easy to come by when we are the ones setting expectations for ourselves.

Even though we have all failed at some point in our life, there is a huge difference between failing and taking on the identity of a failure. Failing at some time in life is inevitable. None of us are perfect and all of us are guilty of sin. If any of us were perfect or free from sin, we would be Jesus. With that said, how do we embrace the fact that it's okay not to be perfect, and at the same time, recognize the truth "I am not a failure?"

**Failure:** *noun* an act or instance of failing or proving unsuccessful; lack of success; nonperformance of something due, required, or expected; a subnormal quantity or quality; an insufficiency; deterioration or decay, especially of vigor, strength, etc.[74]

Recognizing we are not a failure starts with believing in our successes. When we feel successful, thoughts of being a failure lose their power over us. What is true success and where does it come from? Success looks different for everyone, there is no set of standards that can be applied and put into a formula to generate the answer to success.

Knowing the truth that God created each of us for a unique purpose, it would stand to reason that success also looks unique for each one of us. How exactly do we determine our success?

*Who are you to judge the servants of someone else? It is their own Master who will decide whether they succeed or fail. And they will succeed, because the Lord is able to make them succeed. Romans 14:4*

It is God's job to be the judge of our success, not ours. Allowing anything outside of God determine our success gives room for something other than God to become our master. Often times, that other "master" is our self.

After I moved across the country and started allowing God have deeper influence in my life, I continued my tendency of being the keeper of my own success. Sure, it was great to have God provide me with great new opportunities, but greater opportunities came with greater expectations, right? Not quite. Just because we allow God to take over a greater part of our life, does not mean that he gives us a higher set of expectations of generating success.

Even though God didn't expect me to be a "better person," I expected it of myself. Because of my unrealistic expectations of myself, God enabled me to start leading women's ministry with something smaller and within my comfort zone.

The ministry I helped lead began by meeting once a month in the comfort of my own home. The ministry was the same type of women's ministry that I was involved with years prior, so I knew how to organize it. We invited female influencers in the community that my friend had connections with to come speak on a different attributes of being a Godly woman each month. All I had to do was be willing to facilitate the meetings, create an open and inviting space for women to meet in, and welcome the new women who came into my house with open arms—all things I'm good at naturally. The difference was

---

74  *Dictionary.com,* s.v. "Failure," accessed November 1, 2018, https://www.dictionary.com/

that I got to use those gifts in an atmosphere of fulfilling my God-given purpose. Through God's provision, the ministry saw great success throughout my time in graduate school.

This success should not come as a surprise. God desires equally for all of us to be successful in everything we do. There is no question as to whether or not we will succeed when God is our Master—we succeed because God enables us to succeed.

**How has God brought success into past situations when at the time they seemed unsuccessful?**

_____

_____

_____

_____

**What areas do you currently feel unsuccessful in?**

_____

_____

_____

**How might God be able to bring success into those areas?**

_____

_____

_____

_____

We've talked about how God enables us to succeed, but what does that success look like? How can we identify success in our own life?

**Success:** *noun* favorable or desired outcome[75]

Our success does not come from doing a certain task or being in a specific place in life. What a favorable outcome looks like is relative to our place in life at any given time, it's about taking the scenario at hand and coming out of it better than when we started. Elements that go into attaining success are found just as much in our hard seasons as they are when our life goes well. What characteristics can we foster in order to harvest prosperity and success in whatever life throws our way?

> **Submission to God:** *"Submit to God and be at peace with him; in this way prosperity will come to you." Job 22:21 NIV*
>
> **Joy:** *Happy are those who reject the advice of evil people, who do not follow the example of sinners or join those who have no use for God. Instead, they find joy in obeying the Law of the LORD, and they study it day and night. They are like trees that grow beside a stream, that bear fruit at the right time, and whose leaves do not dry up. They succeed in everything they do. Psalm 1:1-3*
>
> **Generosity:** *A generous person will prosper; whoever refreshes others will be refreshed. Proverbs 11:25 NIV*
>
> **Trust:** *The greedy stir up conflict, but those who trust in the LORD will prosper. Proverbs 28:25 NIV*

None of those verses indicate that success and prosperity are optional outcomes. When we live a life filled with peace, joy, generosity, and trust, success and prosperity *will* result.

Moving across the country was the first time I trusted God to be the one who brought success into my life. In order to continue allowing God to be in charge, I had to learn how to get to know him on a deeper level. Forming a deeper relationship with God was the only way to find the success I dreamt of embodying in the form of a women's ministry.

At this point, I knew for a couple of years that God wanted a relationship with me, but I only allowed him to have a part of my trust. I was able to trust where he was taking me, but I was unable to trust what he wanted to do through me. My view on my ability to lead women's ministry was conditional to how much I trusted my own ability to lead, not on how much I trusted God to provide

---

75   *Merriam-Webster's Dictionary and Thesaurus,* Updated Edition, s.v. "Success."

me with everything I needed to succeed and to be a leader. Leading on my own ability felt safe, allowing God to be in control generated fears of failure.

After two years of leading women's ministry in a comfortable state, although very rewarding, God said "time for more." He led me into student ministry, and I felt completely unqualified. I was the girl in high school who only went to church activities for the people, not for God. "High school me" never read the Bible, rarely prayed, and played no role in pursuing God on a deeper level. How could I be an example to people of that age?

Doubts aside, God placed a desire in me to get more involved with the church. I submitted the desire to him and landed in youth ministry. Because I said "yes," God uses me as an example to them. I am the person for them that I didn't know I needed in high school. Failure is not possible when we live a life with God as our Master. When we trust God with our story, success will result, even if it isn't the success we originally thought or imagined.

**What does God want you to trust over to him?**

_____

_____

_____

_____

**In what ways do you see yourself living out submission, joy, generosity, or trust well? What success or prosperity has come as a result?**

_____

_____

_____

_____

_____

**Which of those qualities do you see the most room for improvement on? How can you implement that improvement into your daily routine?**

_____

_____

_____

_____

## Lesson 2: Expectations

What does it mean to perform? Based on the unique skills, circles of influence, and places we spend our time, the people around us observe our performance. Whether it's a one-time performance of a musical, a quarterly performance in school, or a yearly performance in our job, environments where we have certain levels of expectations placed upon us are all very familiar. As the next definition of failure, "nonperformance of something due, required, or expected"[76] states, any time we do not reach the level of expectations placed upon our performance, we have the potential to feel like a failure.

If we are all honest with ourselves, we assign ourselves requirements and expectations to live up to all the time. These expectations wear many different hats. Some of those expectations are realistic, others aren't. Some of them are based on what we think people expect of us, others we place upon ourselves.

To set up our lives for success, we need to make sure that we live based on realistic expectations, expectations aligning with God's plan for our life and not from the world.

**What expectations do you have that were either set by yourself or set by default as a result of your surroundings?**

_____

_____

---

76 *Dictionary.com*, s.v. "Failure," accessed November 1, 2018, https://www.dictionary.com/

_____

_____

**What are expectations you have that were influenced by God?**

_____

_____

_____

_____

**How has the performance of any of those God-influenced expectations led to you viewing yourself as a success?**

_____

_____

_____

_____

Surely, if God created each of us for a purpose, his plan wasn't to create a bunch of failures. We are all familiar with the types of expectations placed upon us both by ourselves and society, but how do those change when we look from a Godly perspective? What requirements does God have for us?

> Then they asked him, "What must we do to do the works God
> requires?" Jesus answered, "The work of God is this: to believe
> in the one he has sent." John 6:28-29 NIV
> Where, then, is boasting? It is excluded. Because of what law?
> The law that requires works? No, because of the law that requires
> faith. Romans 3:27 NIV
> This, then, is how you ought to regard us: as servants of Christ
> and as those entrusted with the mysteries God has revealed.

*Now it is required that those who have been given a trust must prove faithful. 1 Corinthians 4:1-2 NIV*

God has one main requirement of us—to have faith. Life is really good at distracting us from living in the fullness of this requirement. Simply having faith often seems like it's not enough.

Around the same time I entered student ministry, God prompted me to begin preparing for future ministry opportunities in life by telling me to write this book. My original thought back to him sounded like, "You're kidding me. You want *me* to write something other people will read?" No other area in my life had blinded me to my own success more than books. My grade school story was ruled by consistently underperforming in reading, and my college story consisted of getting told by one of my professors that "I didn't know how to grammatically put a sentence together."

I had plenty of faith in God's ability to do good things, but I had little faith in my own ability to read and write in an influential way. God knew my feelings and said, "Perfect, all the more reason for you to have faith in me to get you there. When you lean on me, I will guide you on the right path."

I analyzed what it would take to accomplish writing that book. Talk about intimidating! All of the requirements on the list for successfully writing a book created a whole new arena of opportunity for failure.

**What causes you to think having faith in Jesus isn't enough for us to view yourself as a success?**

_____

_____

_____

_____

**What is a situation you felt successful in? Did faith play a factor in getting you to the point of feeling successful?**

_____

_____

_____

_____

I knew that on my strength and ability alone, I would never reach success in this journey of book writing that God called me to. Nevertheless, because I knew God strongly called me to pursue writing, I had no logical choice but to rely upon my faith in him. I took on the mindset that if God wanted to make it happen, he was going to make my writing successful whether I thought I possessed the proper ability to do so or not. To no surprise at all, he made success happen.

How exactly can we know that simply having faith is enough to bring success? *Happy are those who remain faithful under trials, because when they succeed in passing such a test, they will receive as their reward the life which God has promised to those who love him. James 1:12*

When we place our faith in God, success is the only option. God will never hold back in rewarding our faithfulness to him.

**What has God promised you? How have you seen him come through on those promises?**

_____

_____

_____

_____

**In what ways have you been rewarded from remaining faithful in times of trial?**

_____

_____

_____

_____

## Lesson 3: Sufficiency

Building on the previous lesson, once we become aware of expectations, we go about any method necessary to fulfill those expectations. When we go out to dinner to a 5-star restaurant, we expect high-quality food and service. If that restaurant gives us anything less, they have failed to meet our expectations.

We're all familiar with not meeting expectations. Is there a difference between failing to meet expectations and taking on the identity of a failure? Does the restaurant's failed attempt to meet the expectations we had of their food make the restaurant a failure? Certainly it doesn't, they were rated 5-stars for a reason.

The next two definitions of "failure" speak to this idea of not living up to certain criteria. They are, "a subnormal quantity or quality" and "an insufficiency."[77] Unlike the example of the restaurant serving up sub-par quality, the source of feeling like a failure due to an insufficiency is often not as concrete. What does it take to view ourselves as sufficient enough to fulfill the calling God has for us?

Seeing our sufficiency is related to our ability to see our capability. When we know our capability, we are able to think more highly of ourselves. Since we know God would never create a person to be doomed for failure, we can be sure he provides us with the sufficiency we need to carry out our purpose. The question is, in what form does our sufficiency present itself?

> But he said to me, "My grace is sufficient for you, for my power is made perfect in weakness." Therefore I will boast all the more gladly about my weaknesses, so that Christ's power may rest on me. 2 Corinthians 12:9 NIV

Sufficiency comes in the form of God's grace. Any time we see ourselves as weak, God works both on and in us though his power and grace. God's grace is sufficient for everyone in *all times* and in *all places*. Sufficiency always exists when it comes to God's power. He is capable of doing anything for us and through us.

**How have you recently felt successful due to feeling sufficient?**

_____

_____

---

77  *Dictionary.com*, s.v. "Failure," accessed November 1, 2018, https://www.dictionary.com/

_____

_____

**How have you recently felt like you were failing due to an insufficiency?**

_____

_____

_____

_____

**Have you asked God to give you his grace in your feelings of insufficiency? If so, what was the result? If not, how could you do so right now?**

_____

_____

_____

_____

What does it look like to find sufficiency in the form of grace? How can we know we are finding and receiving sufficiency by his grace? Products of grace include:

**Help:** *Let us then approach God's throne of grace with confidence, so that we may receive mercy and find grace to help us in our time of need. Hebrews 4:16 NIV*

**Strength:** *You then, my child, be strengthened by the grace that is in Christ Jesus, and what you have heard from me in the presence of many witnesses entrust to faithful men who will be able to teach others also. 2 Timothy 2:1-2 ESV*

**Justification:** *God poured out the Holy Spirit abundantly on us through Jesus Christ our Savior, so that by his grace we might be*

*put right with God and come into possession of the eternal life
we hope for. Titus 3:6-7*

God in his grace, sent his son Jesus to this earth to justify the punishment for our sins. This justification gives us the strength needed to carry out God's plan for our lives.

When God prompted me to write this book, two things were very apparent: this book was part of the plan he had for my life, and there was no way I was going to accomplish doing so without his strength and grace along the way. To say I never had feelings of insufficiency while writing this book would be a lie. However, I continued to pursue my writing anyway. I knew that if this was truly God's plan for my life, the strength I needed would be provided along the way. This book was going to be written. Nothing causing feelings of insufficiency would stop me, because I had God and his grace on my side.

**How have you seen God's grace help you overcome your own feelings of insufficiency?**

_____

_____

_____

_____

**How can you use the help and strength you've received from God's grace to help you extend grace to those around you?**

_____

_____

_____

_____

_____

## Lesson 4: Seen vs. Unseen

In the world of accounting, balance sheets have a line item dedicated to depreciation. The reason for this line item is that assets like buildings and equipment lose value over time. The older those assets get, the less they're worth. The likelihood of those assets failing in some way with use over time increases. This concept of failure is seen in the definition stating, "deterioration or decay, especially of vigor, strength, etc."[78]

Unlike every other lesson in this chapter, this angle of failing refers to something which has lost its ability to perform a task with which it was once capable. From the definition of failure, we see one example of this type of failing is through our strength. Looking into the familiar process of aging, the older we get, the more our physical strength deteriorates. Just because our physical strength eventually fails us, does not mean we are being set up for failure. God is very familiar with things like the aging process, and he specifically says we need to find our identity in things that cannot, and will not, decay over time.

*For this reason we never become discouraged. Even though our physical being is gradually decaying, yet our spiritual being is renewed day after day. And this small and temporary trouble we suffer will bring us a tremendous and eternal glory, much greater than the trouble. For we fix our attention, not on things that are seen, but on things that are unseen. What can be seen lasts only for a time, but what cannot be seen lasts forever. 2 Corinthians 4:16-18*

**How are you fixing your eyes on the seen rather than the unseen?**

_____

_____

_____

_____

---

78   *Dictionary.com*, s.v. "Failure," accessed November 1, 2018, https://www.dictionary.com/

**Can you think of an example of how focusing your eyes on the seen world lasted for only a time?**

_____

_____

_____

_____

_____

Anything of the seen world that we fix our eyes on will decay over time. When we base our success off of fixing our eyes onto the things of the seen world, it eventually fails us. How then, do we instead fix our eyes onto the things unseen?

> _Let us give thanks to the God and Father of our Lord Jesus Christ! Because of his great mercy he gave us new life by raising Jesus Christ from death. This fills us with a living hope, and so we look forward to possessing the rich blessings that God keeps for his people. He keeps them for you in heaven, where they cannot decay or spoil or fade away. They are for you, who through faith are kept safe by God's power for the salvation which is ready to be revealed at the end of time. Be glad about this, even though it may now be necessary for you to be sad for a while because of the many kinds of trials you suffer. Their purpose is to prove that your faith is genuine. Even gold, which can be destroyed, is tested by fire; and so your faith, which is much more precious than gold, must also be tested, so that it may endure. Then you will receive praise and glory and honor on the Day when Jesus Christ is revealed. 1 Peter 1:3-7_

The things we receive when we live a life focused on the unseen world will not decay. Failure does not exist when we live our lives rooted in a faith in Jesus. However, no one ever said that living a life of following Jesus is easy. Even God himself said it won't be easy. Sadness and suffering are necessary components of strengthening our faith—a faith more precious than gold.

Going through the process of writing this book was—hands down—one of the hardest things I've ever done in the testing of my faith. Writing has been essential for achieving the intimacy I've desired my entire life. The tears were many, the suffering was great, and I was drawn out of my comfort zone often. I was required to spend a lot more alone time than my extremely extroverted tendencies cared to commit to. I realized I had nowhere near as much trust for God's ability to use my story for his good as I thought I did. I was forced to relive times of past suffering that I couldn't care less to experience again. I put it all on paper with the hope that this book draws everyone who reads it closer to him. I constantly asked, "Why me, God? Cant someone else write this story?" God's answers to those questions were, "Why *not* you?" and "Because this is what I've called you to. I have a specific purpose for you."

Just as God calls me to a specific purpose, he calls *you* to a specific purpose. He wants us to succeed in our purpose so badly, he sacrificed his son Jesus to die for us and allow us to have a relationship with him. A relationship which will never disappoint, always provide, always satisfy, and always be enough.

Wherever you are in life, *never* lose sight that you have a purpose and that you are the *only* one who can fulfill that purpose in the way God designed. Jesus died so God can have a relationship with you—a relationship more intimate than you will ever find with any human being on this earth. What steps will you take to draw closer to him?

**Do you view yourself as being much more precious than gold? If so, how or in what way? If not, what prevents you from doing so?**

_____

_____

_____

_____

_____

**How is your faith currently being tested or purified?**

_____

_____

_____

_____

**What does having a genuine faith in Jesus look like for you?**

_____

_____

_____

_____

Dear God,

I pray against anything causing me to see myself as a failure. Help me to shift my mind away from what the world describes success as and toward what you define success as. Show me ways I can exercise hope, joy, peace, generosity, and trust to bring success into areas of my life where I currently feel defeated. Help me to set more realistic expectations for my life and to see how your love for me and your plans for my life are always enough. Thank you for supplying me with your never-ending sufficient grace at all times. Your grace gives me the strength to overcome feelings of failure and provides me with power in every area of my weaknesses. I confess that all too often I place my hope in the things of this world rather than the unseen world, and ask that you would give me the strength to keep my eyes fixed on you. Thank you for being a God who cannot and will not fail, and for being a God who fights for me and for my success at all times.

In Jesus' name,
Amen

# About the Author

Emily has a passion for reaching out to women and guiding them to living out an identity rooted in truth. After being a rape survivor, she found her life quickly turn away from having everything she thought she wanted and toward feelings of both hopelessness and worthlessness. It was during that time, and being open about her experience, that it became apparent to her just how many other people experience those same feelings and so easily allow things that aren't true about them define them.

Her passion for wanting to take her outreach to women to the next level drove her toward writing this book. She began to identify some of the most popular lies she saw and heard people believing about themselves. From her past experiences, she was able to find new life for herself in living her life for God. For that reason, she uses the Bible as the source of this book to provide truth for people to turn to during any time they may be seeing themselves falling in to the traps of any of these lies.

She lives to share her passion of empowering women to experience the freedom found from living in fullness of God's truth with all who God places in her path. She has spoken to and shared this passion with hundreds of people belonging to various faiths, age groups, and nations. Locally, she serves as a mentor to the next generation and speaks at numerous events in both the faith and sexual assault arenas in the Salt Lake Valley. Globally, she has shared her passions through humanitarian work in eSwatini, Africa, where she has gained a multi-cultural perspective of how the freedom from knowing God's truth manifests in others.

# Call to Action

For more from Emily, visit http://www.emilybernathauthor.com/self-truth-handout and download the free handout including more self truths backed by Biblical references.

CPSIA information can be obtained
at www.ICGtesting.com
Printed in the USA
BVHW080606220819
556519BV00001B/11/P